RETREAT

RETREAT
THE MODERN HOUSE IN NATURE

RON BROADHURST

New York · Paris · London · Milan

FOR D. A. BROADHURST

PREFACE
RON BROADHURST

When I first conceived the idea for this book I had wanted to title it *Retreat: Houses at the Edge of the World*, but my publisher found that to sound more apocalyptic than inviting. However, then and now the prevailing mood of the culture, at least in the United States, seemed to be in a schizophrenic state: on the one hand, weary of our endless war in the Middle East, and on the other, optimistic regarding technological innovation at home (thank you, Apple). And indeed at least one of the projects featured in this book could represent a flight from the realities of twenty-first-century civilization—Fearon Hay's Island Retreat, on Waiheke Island, eleven miles off the coast of New Zealand, with its bunker-like profile, retractable metal screens over glass walls, and impressive array of solar panels.

But as I carried out the process of selecting projects that were among the most responsive to their natural contexts and the most formally and structurally innovative, not to mention the most reasonably recently completed, I discovered that my proposed title would have been a fallacy. The projects that most captured my attention led me to question what constituted the nature of a domestic retreat in the early twenty-first century.

For instance, the two Scandinavian projects in this volume, by Tham & Videgård and Atelier Oslo, are on waterside sites that are not particularly isolated but which offer a context of nearly undisturbed natural beauty, and are distinctly second homes, small in scale and designed specifically as retreats from quotidian life in the city or suburbs. Similarly, Bates Masi + Architects' project in the Hamptons and Peter Rose + Partners' project on Martha's Vineyard could hardly be considered isolated, and the former's natural context could hardly be considered rustic, but both projects exhibit an almost aggressive desire to engage with their surrounding environment, the Rose project by virtue of its uninhibited openness, the Bates Masi project by way of its site-defining boardwalk, which extends like an outstretched arm to an isolated guesthouse built by Andrew Geller in 1962.

Maybe the gold standard of the modern retreat can be found in Bohlin Cywinksi Jackson's Skyline House in Oregon, crowning a steep slope with breathtaking views of the Cascade Mountains, or Rick Joy's Lone Mountain Ranch House, lonesome indeed on a 27,000-acre cattle ranch outside the ghost town of Golden, New Mexico. Coincidentally both of those projects are composed of simple forms and, in the case of the Skyline House, remarkably modest materials. But formal refinement and a deliberate engagement with the natural environment, as well as a fair degree of isolation, perhaps best capture the spirit of *Retreat*.

Such are the conditions of William Reue's project in the woods of upstate New York, where an enigmatic structure with a curved steel front facade evocative of a Richard Serra sculpture and a glass-walled rear facade sits like a jewel box among a phalanx of spruce trees. On the other side of the country, Barbara Bestor's Toro Canyon House is an object lesson in nature tamed, a luxuriously rustic villa overlooking artfully manicured grounds, but set among the wild canyons of Santa Barbara County. The site is idyllic, just outside the small town of Toro Canyon, between Santa Barbara and Los Angeles, yet a world away from either. Up the coast, near Big Sur, Anne Fougeron's Fall House is a tour de force of structural ingenuity and material richness, a gravity-defying essay in copper and glass that clings to a bluff lowering to the ocean until culminating with a cantilevered master bedroom suite. Naturally my publisher selected Fall House to appear on this book's cover.

At some point I had to wonder if a site within a so-called megalopolis—an outdated term that has been bureaucratically deconstructed into smaller "metropolitan statistical areas"—should disqualify certain projects from being included in this volume. Though these census-designated areas are still large enough to expand the urban population of, for example, New York from 8.5 million to 20 million, should the masterfully crafted houses by Allied Works Architecture in Dutchess County and KieranTimberlake in Pound Ridge have been excluded from these pages? Not if one considers a retreat to be defined by the poise a house displays in the company of nature.

OLSON KUNDIG ARCHITECTS
THE PIERRE
SAN JUAN ISLANDS, WASHINGTON

Architect Tom Kundig of the renowned Seattle-based firm of Olson Kundig was presented with a particularly inspiring site for this house near the shore of one of Washington State's San Juan Islands: a place of primordial beauty with sweeping views of a complex system of straits and archipelagos that compose Puget Sound. Rather than setting this house at the site's highest point, Kundig made the bold move of setting the house deep within the rocks that constituted the site's surface, dynamiting into and excavating the site to create a below-grade plinth into which the house would be nestled.

At the entrance, a wood-clad storage box (made with siding reclaimed from a house designed by Lionel Pries, a leading architect in the Pacific Northwest during the early twentieth century) signals a transition from natural context to the house's double-height, glass-clad facade to an open space containing living and dining areas and the kitchen. Tucked just off the kitchen, the master suite features an ample sitting area with access through floor-to-ceiling sliding glass panels to a large terrace with an outdoor fireplace (both it and the fireplace inside were carved from existing stone). In the master bathroom, three polished stone pools function as naturally composed basins. Off the main space, a powder room is carved out of the rock, where a mirror set within a deep oculus reflects natural light into the space.

Contrasting the natural stone that protrudes into many unexpected spaces, the materials composing the house's core structure—mild steel, smooth concrete, and drywall—provide a neutral background against which contemporary artwork, antiques, and custom furnishings are emphasized. Nothing, however, can neutralize the breathtaking views of the bay and surrounding landscape from the living space's floor-to-ceiling wall of windows and the terrace, here accessed by a large pivoting steel and glass door. Fittingly for a part of the country known for its devotion to green practices, the roof is a lush lawn system that collects and recycles water, and the interior flooring was created from crushed pieces of the rock that was excavated during the construction process.

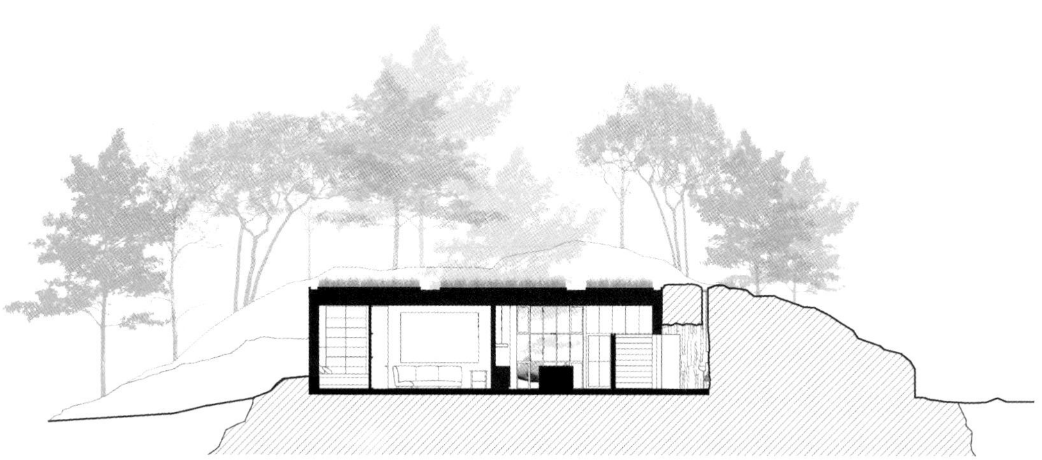

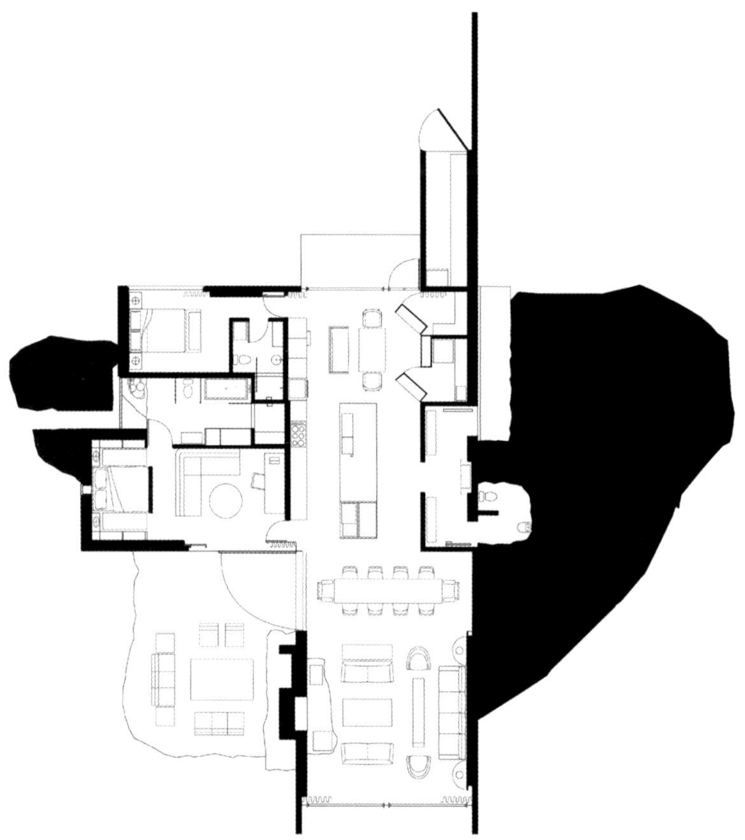

OPPOSITE
Rather than setting the house at the site's highest point, architect Tom Kundig nestled it deep within the rocks that constituted the site's surface.

FOLLOWING PAGES
A large, pivoting steel and glass door opens from the living and dining space and leads to a terrace with outdoor fireplace.

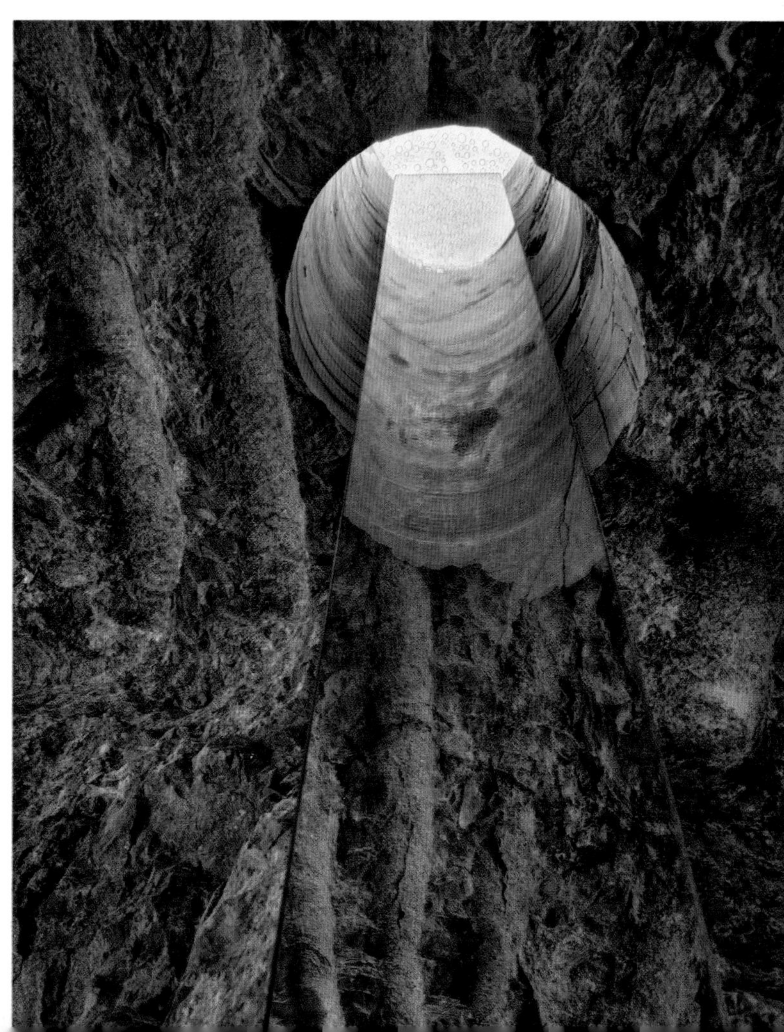

OPPOSITE
A steeping pool in the master bathroom, composed of existing stone from the site, offers a view of Puget Sound.

RIGHT
A powder room is carved out of the rock, where a mirror set within a deep oculus reflects natural light into the space.

PAGES 18 AND 19
The client's collection of contemporary works of art and antique furniture fills the open living and dining space.

PAGES 20 AND 21
Natural stone protrudes throughout the house, as in the fireplace in the living and dining space, which is carved out of existing stone on the site and leveled on top.

SORRY!

FEARON HAY ARCHITECTS
ISLAND RETREAT
WAIHEKE ISLAND, NEW ZEALAND

The firm of Fearon Hay Architects, based in Aukland, New Zealand, and founded by Jeff Fearon and Tim Hay, has developed an impressive portfolio of luxuriously pared-down oceanside houses on remote sites with spectacular views. Yet among these idyllic aeries, Fearon Hay has employed a surprisingly diverse array of structural methods and materials, including monolithic schist, multicolored rough-hewn cement, dark-stained rough-sawn timber, and glass boxes with attenuated structural supports and roofs.

Like these houses, the Island Retreat on Waiheke Island—in New Zealand's Hauraki Gulf, roughly eleven miles off the coast of Aukland—enjoys a paradisiacal setting on a hilltop overlooking the bay across verdant bluffs. However, this house is composed of three main living structures set in an excavated "saddle" that protects the residence from the inhospitable winds that accompany the idyllic site.

Each of the house's three freestanding structures serves a dedicated function: one for living, dining, and kitchen spaces; one for bedrooms; and one for a studio. The arrangement of these structures creates another living space, a surrounded courtyard replete with patios, lawn, a central freestanding firepit, and an adjacent dark-surfaced pool.

With a site endowed with so much drama, including the challenging winds as well as the breathtaking views, the house was conceived by the architects as a camp. Rough concrete structures with retractable glass panels are covered by elegant draped roof planes inspired by lightweight canopies.

The house's bunkerlike profile, modulated as it is by massive glass panels, is further softened by the variety of materials found in each living pavilion, including a smooth stone fireplace and leather sunken seating area in the living space, and veneered timber walls in the bedrooms. Warm-toned wooden furniture and neutral-colored, linen floor-to-ceiling window shades that retract to conceal adjacent walls contribute an additional sense of luxury and comfort within the austere pavilions.

Among the residence's most distinctive features are the open fires: the central fire in the courtyard, the refined walled fireplace in the living space's sunken seating area, and the outdoor fireplace that warms the patio adjacent to the living space. All of these allude to an elemental character that belies the overall modernist structural concept but that perfectly complements the house's ambitious sustainability program, which includes rainwater-harvesting systems and an almost sculptural array of solar panels, minimizing the demands made upon its Edenic setting.

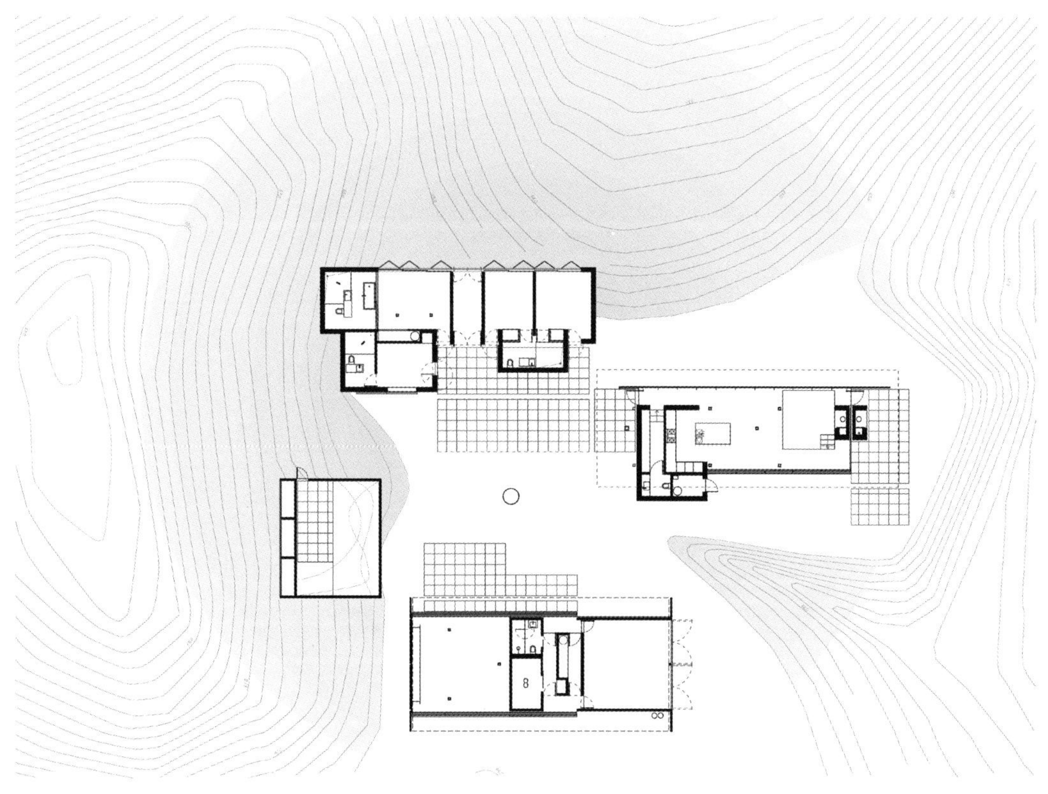

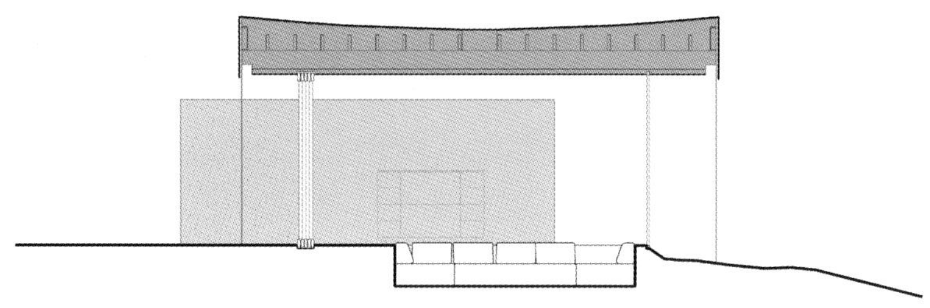

OPPOSITE
The house is composed of separate pavilions, with the main living pavilion composed of an open living, dining, and kitchen space. The austere structure is softened by the warm-toned wooden dining table, a smooth stone fireplace, and a leather sunken seating area.

FOLLOWING PAGES
The main living pavilion is enclosed by massive glass panels on two sides, with this view revealing the size and drama of the sunken seating area.

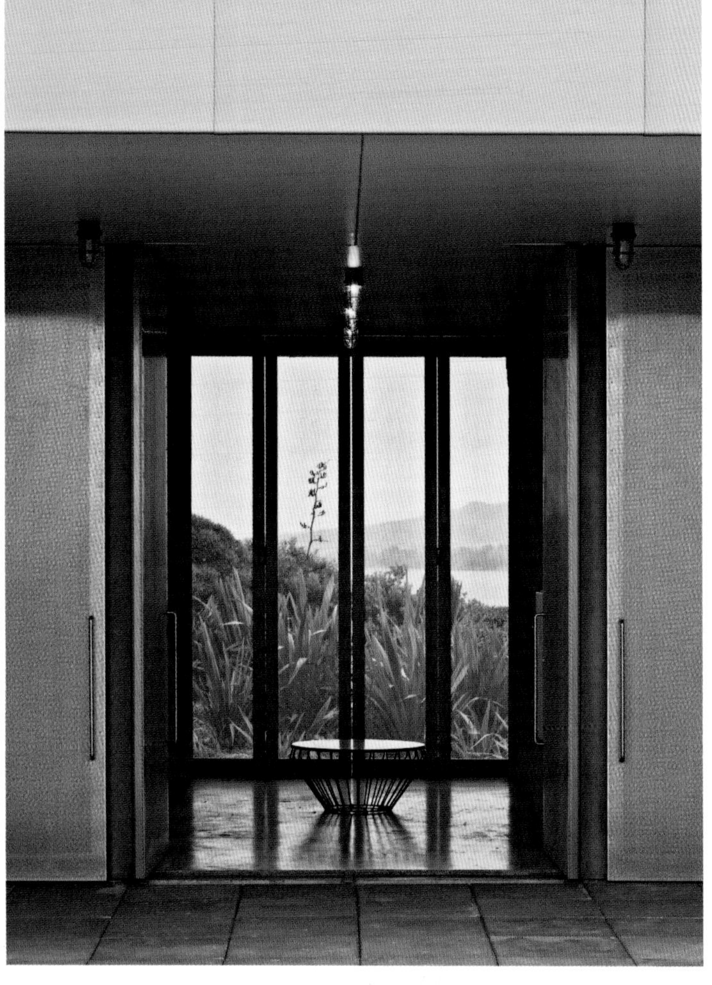

ABOVE LEFT
Bedrooms are accessed from outside; here a breezeway is flanked by the door to the master bedroom suite on the left and the door to another bedroom on the right.

BELOW LEFT
The master bathroom features a steeping tub and, behind the sink, a large, open shower.

ABOVE OPPOSITE
Three of the four bedrooms, including the master bedroom suite, feature protective metal panels, behind which are floor-to-ceiling glass sliding panels.

BELOW OPPOSITE
The master bedroom features veneered timber walls, as do all the other bedrooms.

PAGES 30 AND 31
The house's separate pavilions surround a courtyard that features patios, a lawn, and a central freestanding fire pit. The adjacent dark-surfaced pool is in the foreground.

PAGES 32 AND 33
The patio adjacent to the main living space features an outdoor fireplace as well as breathtaking views of New Zealand's Hauraki Gulf.

HERBST ARCHITECTS
UNDER POHUTUKAWA
PIHA, NEW ZEALAND

When architects Lance and Nicola Herbst moved to New Zealand from South Africa, they were immediately fascinated by the local building type known as a bach—a modest beach cottage constructed from timber and corrugated iron. This fascination led them to engage in a number of projects that referred back to the classic bach with timber construction. The latest of these, called Under Pohutukawa, in Piha, New Zealand, a small coastal municipality, takes its name from another New Zealand fixture, the pohutukawa, a tree of great symbolic significance to the Maori and of great pride to New Zealanders in general. Protected by many local authorities, including Piha, the tree created a singular challenge for the architects, who had to build on a site that was part of a belt of beachfront forest and therefore covered with pohutukawa.

This challenge was relieved somewhat by the easygoing nature of the clients, who simply requested three bedrooms, plenty of light, and the ability to open the house up in summer. Beyond that, the Herbsts were free to what they wanted, and to determine what that was, they looked to the trees themselves as inspiration for the structure's construction as well as siting. Their first priority was to remove as few trees as possible, leading them to decide on a two-story structure to minimize the house's footprint, and also to construct the house's foundation as a series of raised piles rather than a single concrete slab in order to protect the network of roots that would remain under the built structure even after the clearing of the minimum number of trees (specifically four in this case).

Once the siting of the house was determined, the focus turned to the interior of the house, which is organized around a large, open, double-height kitchen, dining, and living space with two of its four sides composed entirely of glass. The large glass panes also extend partway up the roof, creating a continuous skylight that extends along the entire width of the living and dining space, making an outsize light box, necessary to allow as much natural illumination as possible into a house covered by a canopy of pohutukawa trees. Additionally the other three sides of the space feature clerestory windows.

Adjacent to this remarkably open volume is a pair of two-story volumes devoted to the house's private zones, accommodating three bedrooms (one on the first floor and two on the second) and a garage. A narrow mezzanine overlooking the living and dining space connects these two volumes, which are clad on the exterior in dark cedar boards arranged in a series of battens, while the interior walls are finished entirely in natural cedar, whose light warmth offers a naturally elegant respite from the dense forest outside.

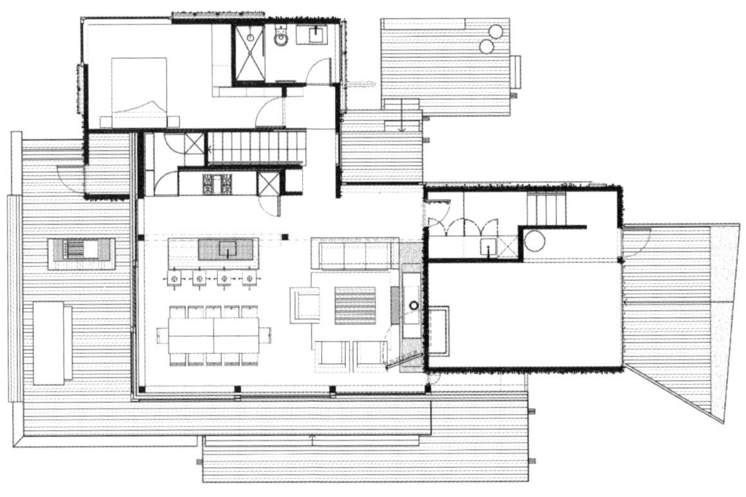

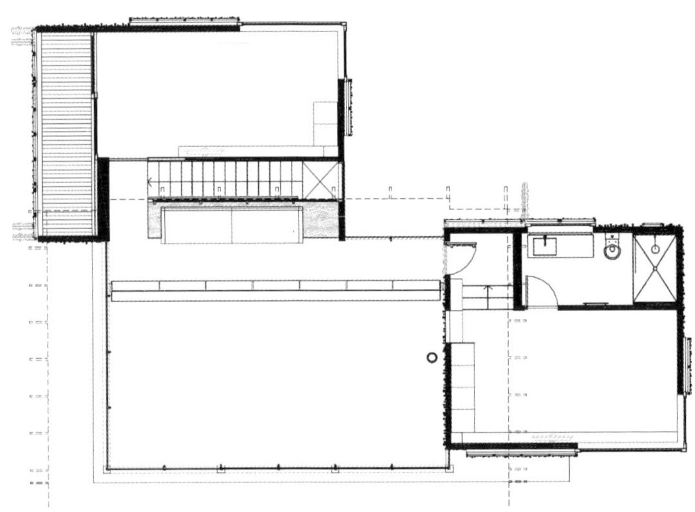

OPPOSITE
The house is clad in dark cedar boards arranged in a series of battens. On the house's second level, these boards slide to completely open a corner of the master bedroom.

FOLLOWING PAGES
A mezzanine runs along one edge of the double-height main living space, seen from both sides of the house here.

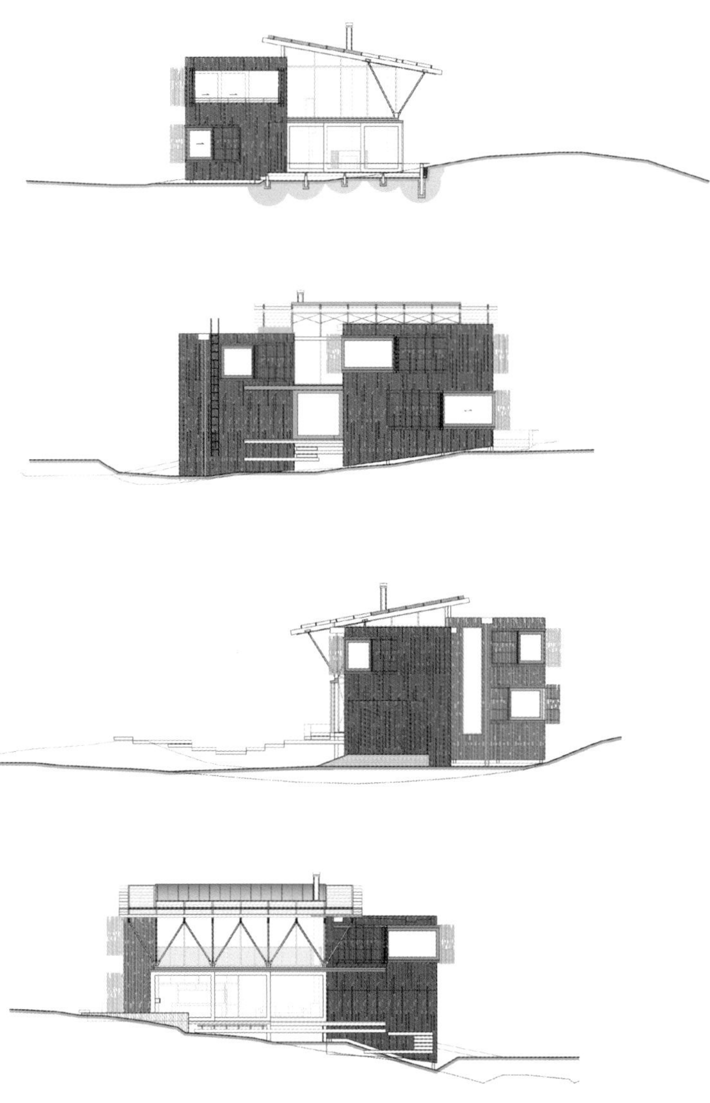

LEFT
The main living space is composed of the kitchen, at left, and open living and dining areas.

FOLLOWING PAGES
The large glass panes enclosing the main living space extend partway up the roof, creating a continuous skylight that spans the entire width of the room.

HER ROYAL HIGHNESS
Queen
King

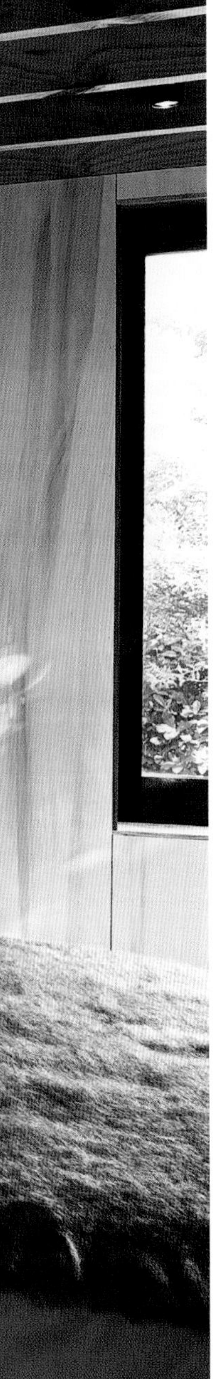

LEFT
The master bedroom suite.

ABOVE RIGHT
A glimpse into the master bedroom, where built-in wardrobes can be seen in the background.

BELOW RIGHT
The bedroom on the lower level features a short corridor lined with bookshelves.

PAGES 46 AND 47
The heart of the house, the double-height main living space, is characterized by openness and warmth.

PAGES 48 AND 49
The entire house seems securely integrated among the revered pohutukawa trees.

CARL TURNER ARCHITECTS
OCHRE BARN AND STEALTH BARN
CAMBRIDGESHIRE, UK

With the Ochre Barn, Carl Turner Architects have converted a derelict Norfolk barn to create a multiuse series of spaces. It is intended as part home, part workplace. The main threshing barn accommodates the main public areas of the building; the longer wing forms a sequence of bedrooms and bathrooms. The architects preserved the building's exterior and inserted a new lining to the interior of existing walls. Doors and windows have been set back to this line to emphasize the thickness of the walls and expose the beautiful brick details. The interior has been left open where possible, with the architects treating it as a landscape where cellular spaces function as buildings within buildings. The spaces between these overscaled furniture pieces and "pods" operate at a more intimate scale. The materials chosen for the interior are largely industrial: power-floated concrete, reclaimed pitch pine boards, and particleboard.

Stealth Barn sits adjacent to and complements Ochre Barn. This addition was to provide a self-contained unit that could equally act as a guesthouse, studio, or meeting place: a retreat that would serve as a place of work and home without compromising the experience of either. The Stealth Barn is sited perpendicularly to the older structure of the Ochre Barn, creating an area with a sense of enclosure, a garden space that complements the barns' isolated fens setting.

Yet while Stealth Barn's design acknowledges the form of the traditional barn, it is also an enigmatic, sharply defined black volume. Its exterior is confined to a restricted material palette, devoid of detail, and built to withstand its exposed position in the landscape.

Inside, the starkness of the building's exterior is countered by the warmth of the particleboard that completely surfaces the walls and ceilings. This bold use of material creates an interior landscape with spaces simply delineated within a semiopen plan to form a series of compartments. The arrangement of these spaces into simple pockets was key to facilitating the barn's multifunctional use in which any one space can become a bedroom, a meeting room, a dining room, or a studio space, all without conveying a profile that is either strictly commercial or domestic.

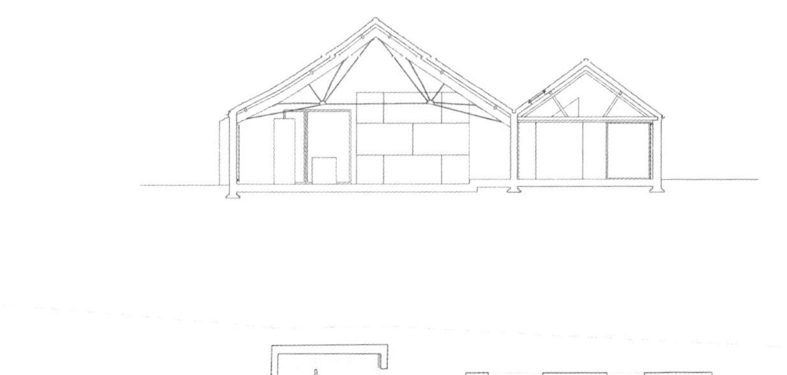

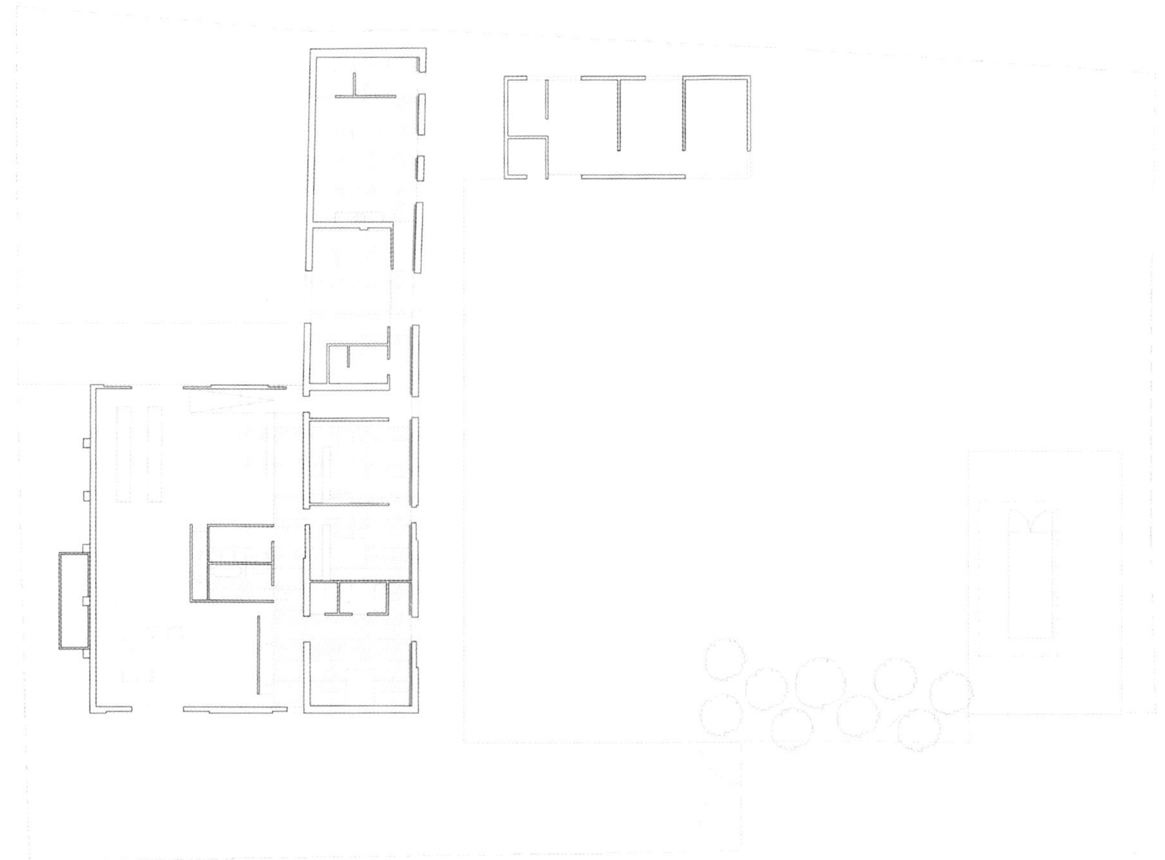

OPPOSITE
While Stealth Barn's design acknowledges the form of the traditional barn, it is nonetheless a sharp black mass with a restricted material palette, devoid of fussy detail, and built to withstand its exposed position in the landscape.

PAGES 54 AND 55
The architects treated the interior of the Ochre Barn like a landscape, where the large, open space of the main threshing barn is modulated by overscaled furniture pieces and "pods."

PAGES 56 AND 57
The materials chosen for the interior of the Ochre Barn are largely industrial: power-floated concrete, reclaimed pitch pine boards, and particleboard.

THORPE ST. ANDREWS
TUCKSWOOD
HEARTSEASE
VULCAN ROAD
RELIEF
PRIVATE
SPECIAL
EXCURSION
NORWICH BUS STATION
AYLSHAM
BACTON
BLAKENEY
BLOFIELD
CATFIELD
COLTISHALL
CROMER
CAWSTON
EAST RUSTON
FREETHORPE

DONALD JUDD

CATFIELD
CROMER
CAWSTON
HEMSBY

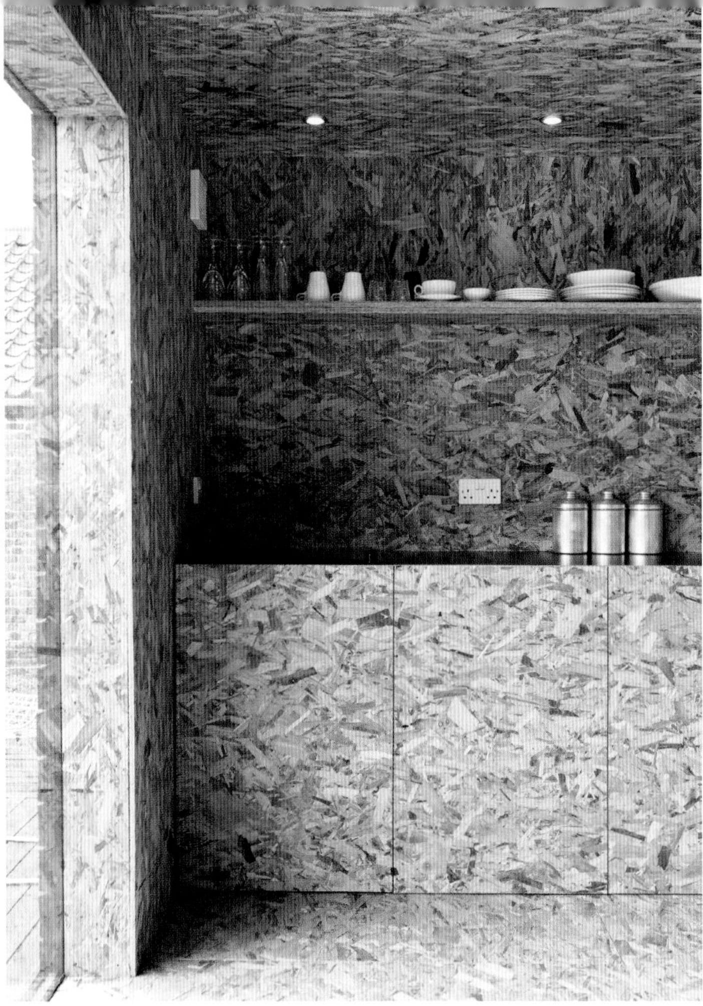

LEFT
In the Stealth Barn the starkness of the building's exterior is countered by the warmth of the particleboard that completely surfaces the walls and ceilings.

BELOW
The Stealth Barn's spaces are simply delineated within a semiopen plan to create a series of multifunctional compartments.

OPPOSITE ABOVE AND BELOW
The longer wing of the Ochre Barn forms a sequence of bedrooms and bathrooms. The master bedroom, above, features its own wood-burning stove.

FOLLOWING PAGES
The longer wing of the Ochre Barn, with the Stealth Barn in the foreground. In the background can be seen the roof of the main threshing barn belonging to the Ochre Barn.

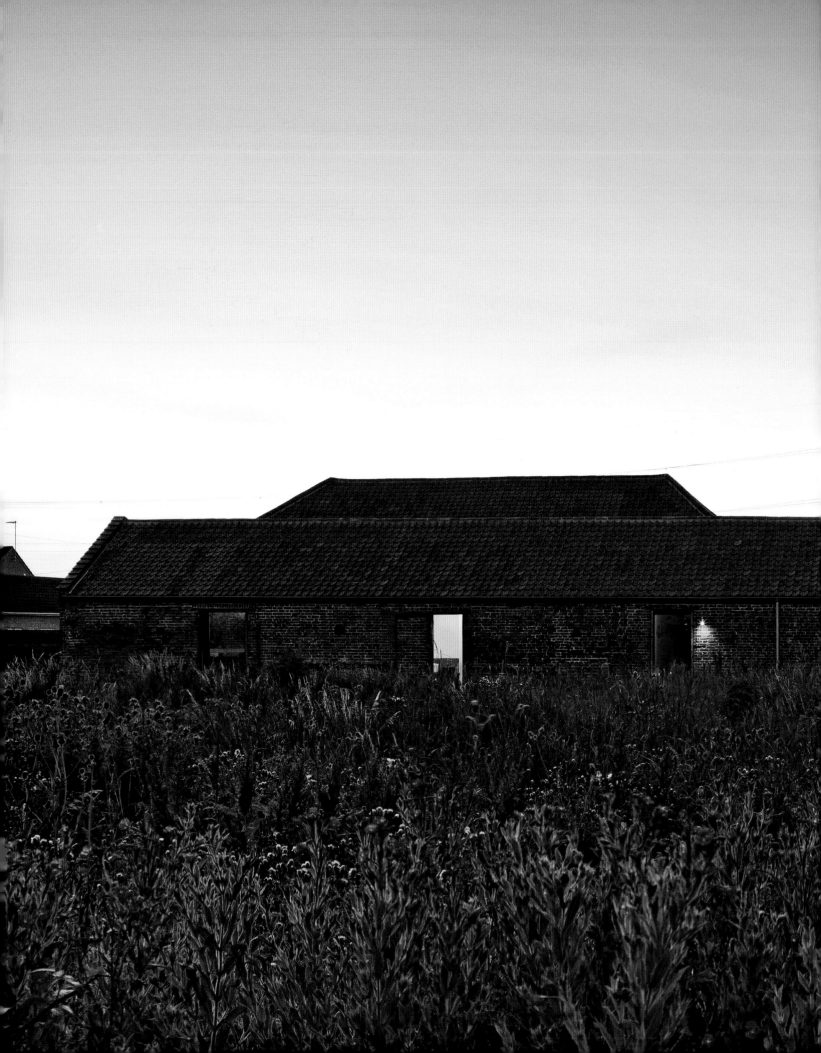

ALLIED WORKS ARCHITECTURE
DUTCHESS COUNTY MAIN RESIDENCE
DUTCHESS COUNTY, NEW YORK

Allied Works Architecture, headed by Brad Cloepfil, has an identity firmly rooted in its West Coast locale, thanks in large part to the iconic headquarters that the firm designed for Wieden + Kennedy in its hometown of Portland. But far from being a local wonder, Allied Works can claim a series of high-profile projects throughout the United States, including St. Louis's Contemporary Art Museum, the Clyfford Still Museum in Denver, the Seattle Art Museum, the University of Michigan Museum of Art, as well as the planned National Music Centre of Canada, in Calgary. And one of the most talked about of these projects, the Museum of Arts and Design, brought Cloepfil to New York, where in 2004 he established an East Coast outpost.

The move east introduced the firm to a once-in-a-lifetime opportunity to create a series of residential structures, art facilities, and outbuildings for a family with a significant contemporary art collection. In collaboration with landscape architect Michael Van Valkenburgh, the architects produced a master plan for the four-hundred-acre site in upstate New York, determining the locations of roads and buildings as well as areas for an extensive collection of installation art and sculpture, not to mention a site-specific video installation by Doug Aitken entitled *Light House*, a 360-degree series of projections against the houses' complex array of facades.

The first building, a guesthouse, was completed in 2007, followed by the so-called Art Barn in 2008, and the main residence in 2012. The entire compound is set among the rolling hills of the Hudson River Valley, with the main residence sited at a meadow's edge, which provides panoramic views of the adjacent valley and range of hills beyond. The main residence takes a particularly complex form, what the architects call an "orthogonal helix," in which the house's two main levels follow opposing radial, or pinwheel, plans. This complex organization creates opportunities for intersection between the two levels, such as the double-height living room and family room at opposite ends of the house; the complex plan also allows for two large terraces on the second level and two covered outdoor courtyards on the first level.

The house's structure of attenuated steel and expansive glass and opaque panels allows for varying degrees of transparency, with clear and etched glass panels mediating light and view, and completely opaque panels providing total privacy where required. The exterior panels also operate as screens against which Aitken's video installation is projected, transforming the house's facade from a formidable cluster of built volumes on the landscape into a brilliantly colored and dynamic site of ambiguous shapes and dimensions.

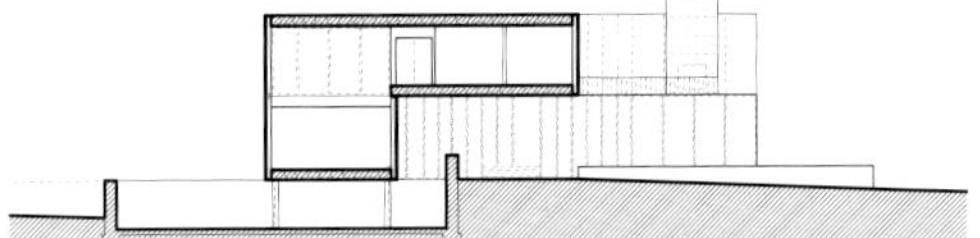

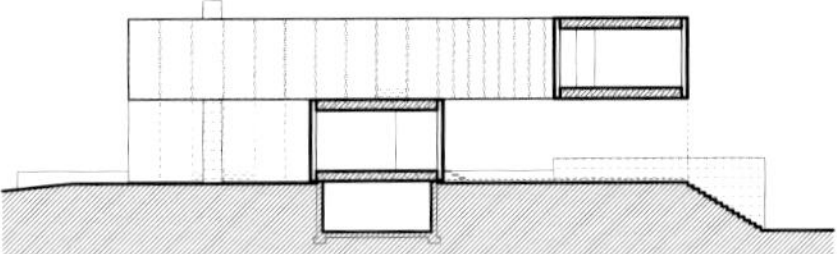

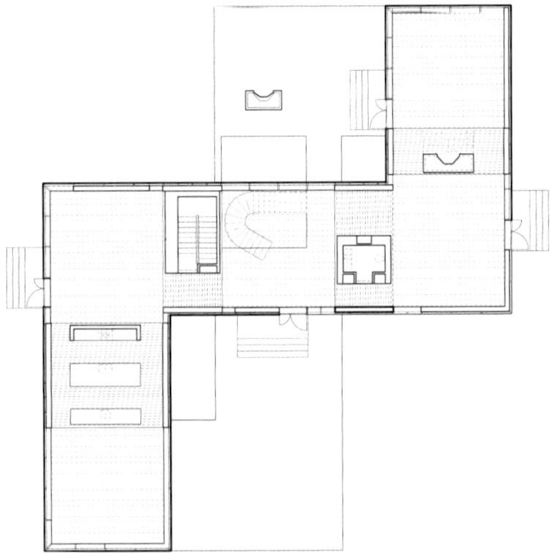

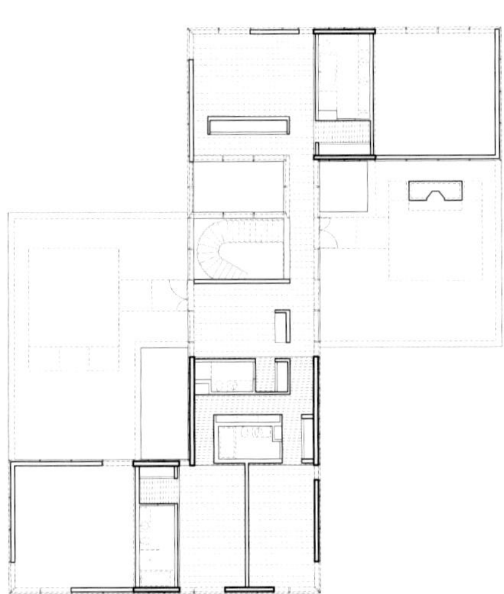

OPPOSITE
The double-height living room, like the rest of the house, is a venue for the clients' extensive collection of contemporary art.

FOLLOWING PAGES
The house is composed of attenuated steel and expansive glass and opaque panels, with the latter acting as screens against which a site-specific video installation by Doug Aitken entitled *Light House* is projected.

OPPOSITE AND BELOW
The house's glass and opaque panels allow for varying degrees of transparency, with clear and etched glass panels mediating light and view.

FOLLOWING PAGES
At the front of the house, the family room, adjacent to an expansive open kitchen with two islands, opens completely to the pool terrace, views of which also greet visitors approaching the house's main entrance.

BELOW AND OPPOSITE
Throughout the house, corners enclosed with floor-to-ceiling glass panels offer private nooks from which to enjoy sylvan views.

PAGES 74 AND 75
The house's complex form, which the architects call an "orthogonal helix," is evident in this rear view of the entrance hall, where a dramatic curved, floating staircase can be glimpsed through the window (page 74), and which can be seen more directly through the house's front door (page 75).

PAGES 76 AND 77
The main entrance is a microcosmic representation of the house as a whole, with its alternating transparent and opaque panels, its semitransparent doors, the sculpture to the left, and the cluster of attenuated steel columns to the right.

BERCY CHEN STUDIO
EDGELAND HOUSE
AUSTIN, TEXAS

Austin-based firm Bercy Chen Studio, led by Belgian Thomas Bercy and Taiwanese-Australian Calvin Chen, has demonstrated a commitment to environmentally sustainable design since its founding in 2001. In addition to issues of sustainability, the firm's work is informed by vernacular precedents from various cultures, whether Islamic, Indian, African, or Pre-Columbian, while maintaining respect for their projects' environmental context, whether urban or rural. For the Edgeland House, the architects took as their point of inspiration the Native American pit house, a structure that was partially dug into the ground. This strategy takes advantage of the surrounding earthen mass to help maintain comfortable temperatures year round, a strategy amplified by the construction of a green roof, which is another significant source of insulation.

The house is visible only as a narrow slice through a hillside, with its seven-foot-deep excavation and dense green roof sheltering two separate pavilions, with an outdoor corridor in between. These two pavilions contain all of the house's interior spaces, with one pavilion dedicated to living, dining, and kitchen spaces, and the other to a pair of bedrooms. The facades of both pavilions, which face the central outdoor walkway and an adjacent courtyard and triangular pool, are clad from floor to peaked roof in reflective glass.

In fact, sharp angles and peaks characterize the formal profile of the house, which is approached down a wide, angular staircase, into a small entry courtyard, and through the central outdoor corridor, which is compressed on both sides by the structures of the two pavilions, each featuring sharply angled outdoor roofs that provide shaded terrace space. This sequence culminates in the large rear terrace and triangular pool, which forms an arrowhead-like pinnacle to the house's overall plan.

Each space—living, kitchen/dining, and both bedrooms—is entered through its own door from the outdoor corridor or courtyards, with the door to the kitchen and dining space functioning as a de facto main entrance. All of the indoor spaces benefit from a combination of energy-saving and environmentally sustainable strategies beyond the insulation provided by the below-grade foundation and thick green roof—including multiple advanced hydronic, or water transfer, systems that supply heating, ventilating, and air-conditioning (HVAC). Additionally, the Lady Bird Johnson Wildflower Center collaborated to reintroduce more native species of plants and wildflowers to the house's site, including its roof, further preserving the local ecosystem.

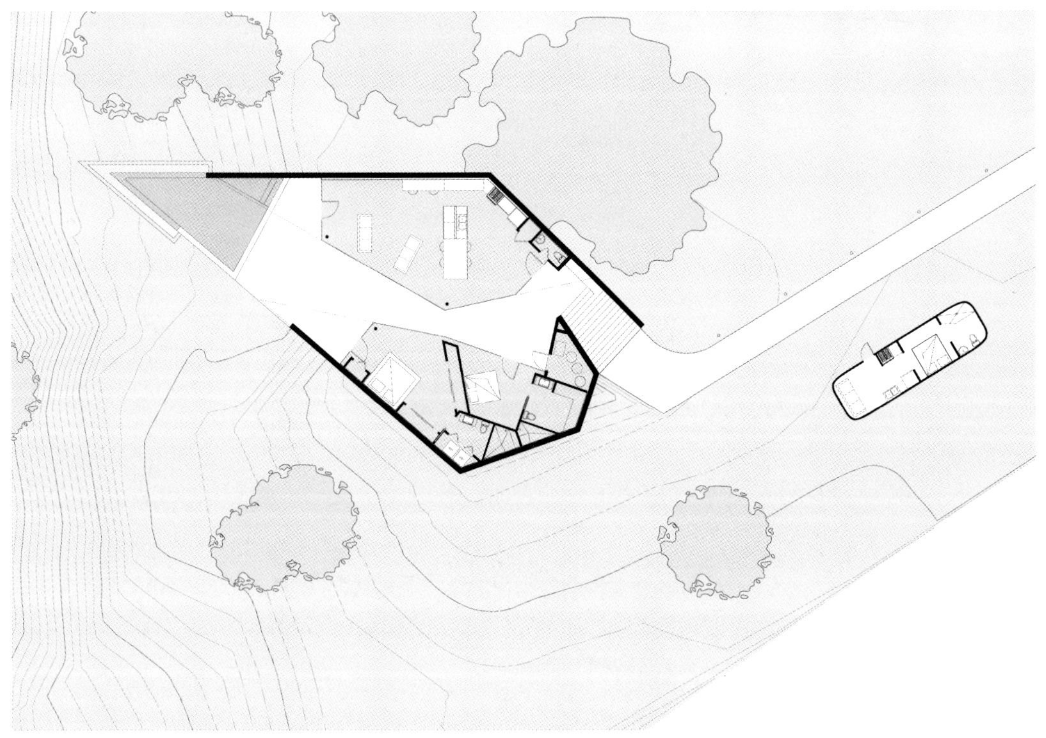

OPPOSITE
The house is approached down a wide, angular staircase, seen here from the living area past the kitchen counter, into a small entry courtyard, which is flanked by the angular structures of the two pavilions.

FOLLOWING PAGES
The architects' inspiration from the Native American pit house, which was partially dug into the ground, takes advantage of the surrounding earthen mass to help maintain comfortable temperatures year round, a strategy amplified by the construction of a green roof, which is another significant source of insulation.

ABOVE OPPOSITE
Another view of the entry stairs, which descend the house's seven-foot-deep excavation into the site's hillside.

BELOW OPPOSITE
The house's two pavilions feature sharply angled outdoor roofs that provide shaded terrace space. Beyond is a large, open terrace leading to the arrowhead-like triangular pool.

PAGES 86 AND 87
The pavilion to the east comprises an open kitchen and living space. The kitchen's stainless-steel countertop extends in sculptural fashion to provide dining space.

PAGES 88 AND 89
While the eastern pavilion (left) provides open living space, the pavilion to the west (right) is composed of two bedrooms, each with its own outdoor entrance.

BARBARA BESTOR
TORO CANYON HOUSE
SANTA BARBARA COUNTY, CALIFORNIA

Architect Barbara Bestor's name has become practically synonymous with Los Angeles, and not just because of the enormous popularity of her book *Bohemian Modern: Living in Silver Lake*, which—by featuring not only her own work but that of her colleagues as well as some classic early- and mid-twentieth-century modernist landmarks—illustrated the architecture of Silver Lake while capturing the spirit of the place. Her reputation as an architect immediately identifiable with L.A. is equally earned by a body of work that comprises residential projects not only in Silver Lake but throughout and around the city, including Eagle Rock, Venice Beach, and Topanga Canyon, as well as commercial projects for such high-profile clients as Trina Turk, Stüssy, and Beats by Dre.

For this getaway on a pristine hilltop site near Montecito, adjacent to national parkland, Bestor's strategy was one of slow revelation and discovery of first the house and then the spectacular view. The road, which had to be built for access, brings the visitor to a point below the house, where a formal stair leads up to the entry sequence. The structure is organized around a central courtyard, which not only provides outdoor space for entertaining but also serves to protect the outdoor space from the region's strong winds.

Inside, a forty-foot-wide horizontal floor-to-ceiling wall of fully retractable windows provides views from the dining room to the dramatic linear swimming pool and the dazzling landscape beyond. The expansive room is anchored by a massive, thick stone wall housing an indoor fireplace to warm the dining hall and, on the opposite side, an outdoor fireplace to warm the central courtyard, effectively creating an outdoor living room. Straddling the dining hall at one end is a nooklike living room, off of which is the master bedroom wing, which features a yoga studio that opens completely to an enclosed courtyard; at the other end of the dining hall is an open kitchen, centered around an island counter of formidable proportions, and off of which another wing contains two bedrooms and a sumptuous cocoon of a media room.

The rough and very thick concrete walls, custom color-mixed to match the dark red and brown tones of the earth at the site, form a rugged shell that is punctuated by massive single-paned windows framed by rich-colored Alaskan cedar. The inner shell's warm wood and windows into the protected courtyards create a retreat from the vigorous environment.

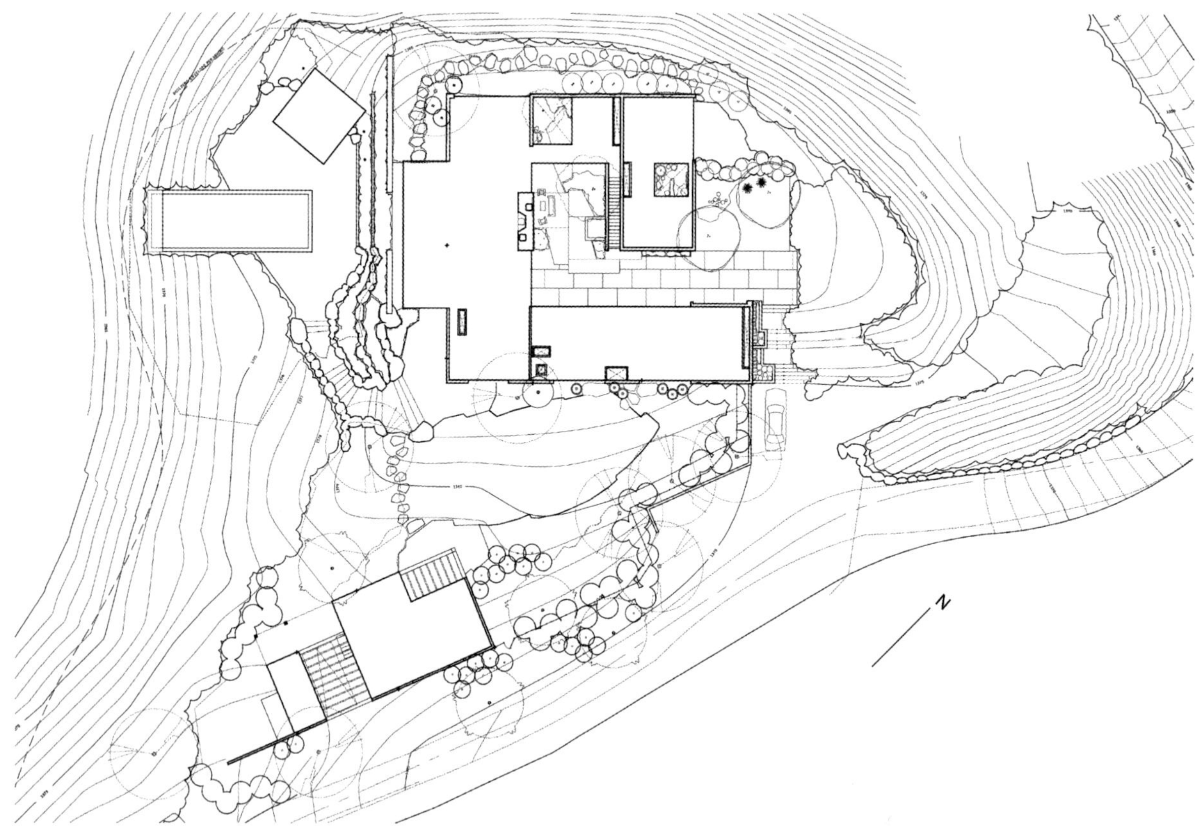

OPPOSITE
From the covered terrace a rustic staircase winds around two rows of landscaped terraces to the pool, the geometric beauty of which complements rather than distracts from the breathtaking landscape beyond.

FOLLOWING PAGES
The covered terrace at the rear of the house is accessed from the massive dining room at the house's center by a forty-foot-wide horizontal floor-to-ceiling wall of fully retractable windows. A separate guesthouse is in the background.

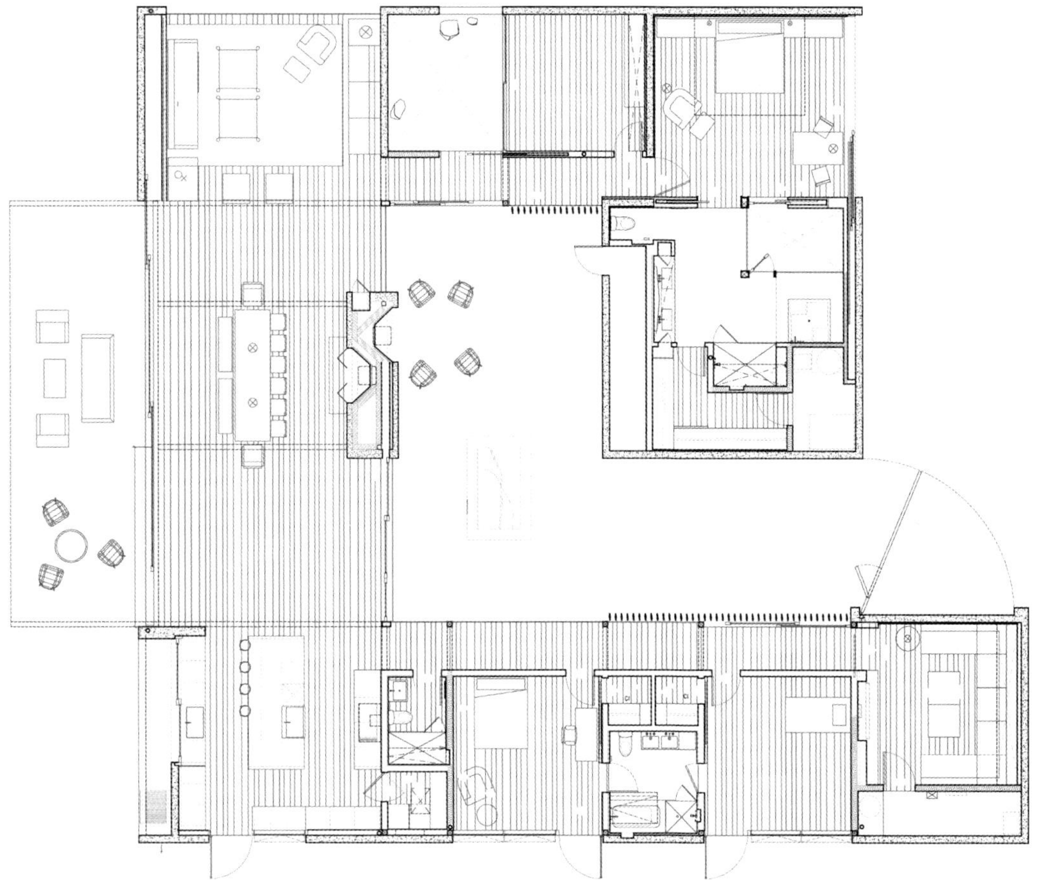

OPPOSITE
The central dining room is flanked on either side by the kitchen to the east, and the living room, seen here, to the west. The west-facing wall of glass offers spectacular views of the sunset.

OPPOSITE
The central courtyard around which the house is organized provides outdoor space for entertaining that is protected from the region's strong winds.

ABOVE RIGHT
On either side of the stone fireplace wall, massive glass panels—framed by rich-colored Alaskan cedar—completely open onto the central courtyard.

BELOW RIGHT
A digitally patterned solar shade gives the pool house maximum shade by following the direction of the sun.

ABOVE AND BELOW LEFT
Massive wood-framed glass panels are installed throughout the house. In the master bedroom, seen here, these glass panels slide open to a secluded hillside terrace.

OPPOSITE
The kitchen is immediately adjacent to the dining room, at the end directly opposite the living room. Its eastern exposure fills the space with morning light.

PAGES 102 THROUGH 105
An expansive dining room is the spatial nucleus of the house, with access to the central courtyard on one side (pages 102 and 103) and to the expansive terrace on the other side (pages 104 and 105).

Eat

BOHLIN CYWINSKI JACKSON
SKYLINE HOUSE
BEND, OREGON

Known for such high-profile projects as the Apple Store on New York's Fifth Avenue and the headquarters for Pixar Animation Studios, Seattle-based architecture firm Bohlin Cywinski Jackson (which also has offices in San Francisco, Philadelphia, Pittsburgh, and Wilkes-Barre, Pennsylvania) demonstrates in its modest Skyline House that great richness can be achieved through the use of affordable materials. The house is sited on the edge of a woodland plateau, with breathtaking views of the Cascade Mountains to the west. From the valley below, the structure looks like a long, attenuated strip composed of metal and glass. Its modest profile on the horizon is fully in keeping with the clients' request for a relatively modest structure that would give them an intimate experience of the surrounding landscape.

To achieve what the clients wanted, the architects decided to use prefabricated materials, including ceiling trusses and plywood and fiber-cement panels, all of which are relatively low cost. The trusses are set up in a rigid series four feet apart, creating a modular organizational system for the house. The use of economical, prefabricated materials was seen as an opportunity to develop an expressive architecture within 2,080 square feet of living space. Between the roof of ACX exterior plywood and interior ceilings of smooth-grained plywood, a gap provides space for insulation. Inside, in addition to the finished plywood ceiling panels, plywood beams are attached to the metal trusses, and laminated wood columns compose the interior frame for the west-facing wall of insulated aluminum and glass panels. The fiber-cement panels provide cladding for the east-facing walls, which are punctuated by long, narrow window bays.

A bridge clad in green fiber cement panels provides an impressive entry sequence. Upon entering the house, the first views of the Cascade Mountain peaks are visible through floor-to-ceiling glass panels, beyond which lies an outdoor deck covered by the entire structure's single roof span. Living and sleeping spaces are arranged in a linear fashion, with a corridor on the east side of the house, flanked by storage spaces and a long children's desk. The corridor leads to the house's three bedrooms, with the master bedroom placed at the northernmost end of the house. Here spectacular views are met through two walls of glass, one of which accesses a narrow, isolated deck that extends out to a cliff's edge and an unrivaled mountain view.

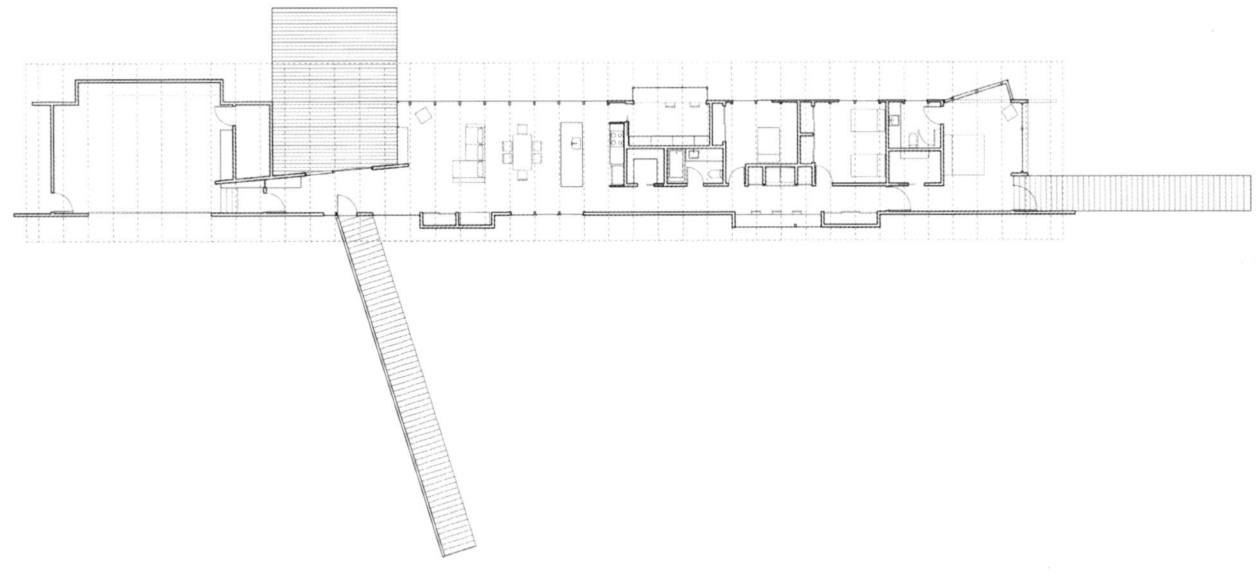

OPPOSITE
Skyline House is a long, slender structure organized on a four-foot module, establishing a rigorous but delicate structural rhythm for the building and maximizing the use of prefabricated materials.

FOLLOWING PAGES
A neon green bridge, one railing of which can be seen in the extreme foreground, marks the approach to the house, which is clad in pre-finished fiber cement panels.

UTZON

ABOVE
Insulated aluminum windows are attached to exposed laminated wood columns, creating an expansive yet economical wall of glass in the open living and dining space.

FOLLOWING PAGES
Throughout the house the ceiling is composed of a series of open web trusses combined with wood framing to form broad overhangs and space for insulation, while plywood is attached to the trusses as a finished ceiling.

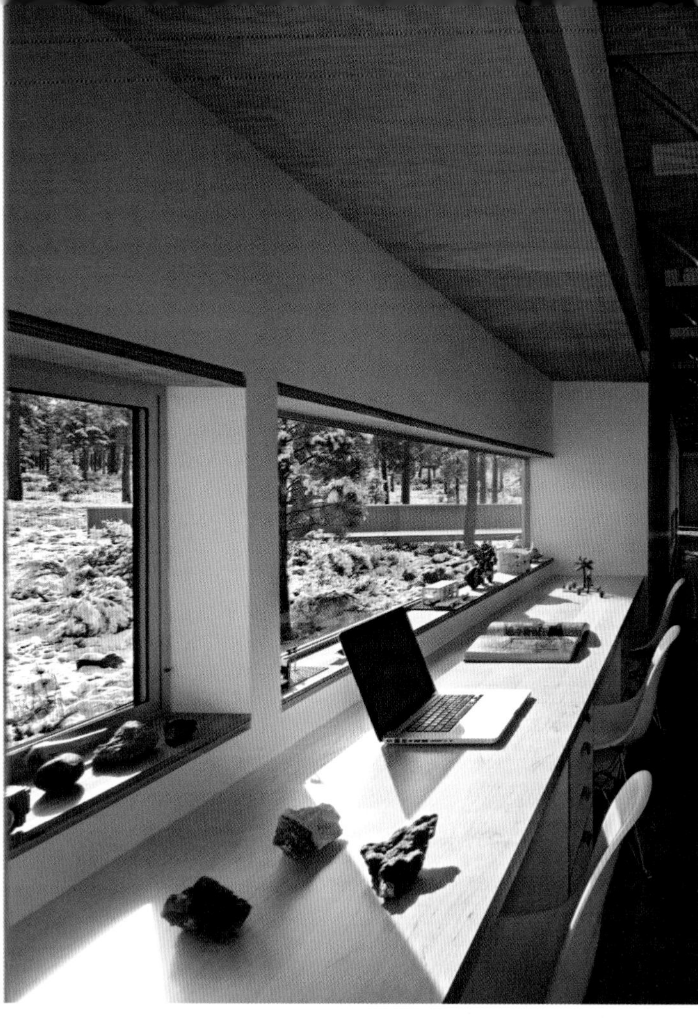

ABOVE LEFT
The bedrooms are organized in a linear fashion off a single corridor, the opposite side of which accommodates a long desktop and space for storage.

BELOW LEFT
Occupying the northernmost end of the house, the master bedroom enjoys spectacular views through two walls of glass.

OPPOSITE
The front door to the house, next to the fire-engine-red panel in the background, leads to an entry corridor with immediate access to a covered terrace, which steps down to an exposed terrace.

RICK JOY
LONE MOUNTAIN RANCH HOUSE
GOLDEN, NEW MEXICO

Rick Joy, based in Tuscon, Arizona, has gained a reputation as an architect's architect due the simultaneous aesthetic integrity and variety demonstrated over the course of his career since the establishment of his firm in 1993. His projects—whether one of multiple houses in Arizona, a loft in New York, a farmhouse in Vermont, the Amangiri Resort Hotel and Spa in Utah, or the Princeton Transit Plaza—employ an astonishing variety of materials and forms to, as Joy himself has stated, "create architecture that is regionally sympathetic and well grounded in the context and community of its place."

The design of the Lone Mountain Ranch, an isolated six-bedroom family retreat on a 27,000-acre cattle ranch in the high desert landscape of New Mexico, takes its cue from the 360-degree views of distant mountain ranges that surround its site. The deceptively simple, shedlike profile of the house belies a complex, though rational, interior plan, which modulates light, shade, and views beneath a single corrugated sheet-metal hip roof. (A hidden wooden deck on the roof provides the ideal stargazing venue for the client, an amateur astronomer.)

Beneath the utilitarian profile of the roof, at either end of the house two bedroom wings, clad in dark-stained wood, are separated by a central space enclosed by floor-to-ceiling glass panels on both sides and comprising the kitchen and living and dining spaces. The south-facing glass wall opens onto an expansive outdoor wooden deck that operates as a large niche beneath the monolithic roof, shielding the window wall from southern exposure to the desert heat.

The simplicity of the main central living space's plan is countered by the relatively complex but precise organization of the two bedroom wings. The wood-clad volume to the east accommodates five bedrooms, two with luxuriously proportioned en suite bathrooms, as well as ample service space. The volume to the west comprises the master suite, which includes two separate office spaces and a refreshingly cozy media room.

Photograph Peter O[illegible]i[illegible]ie

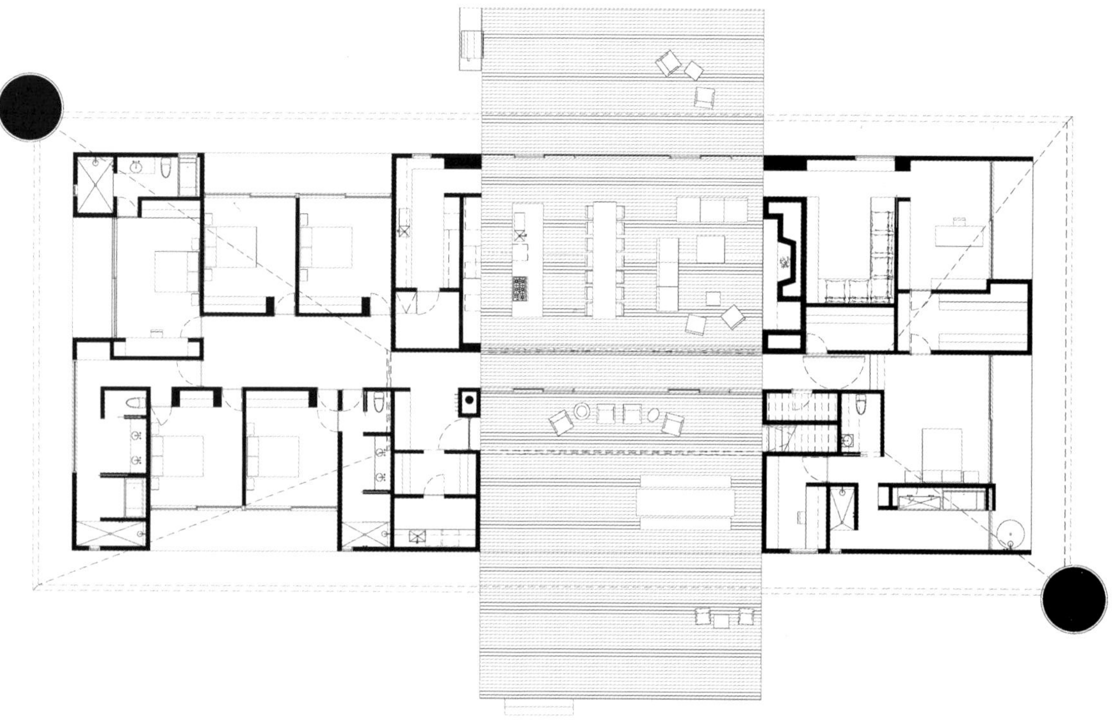

OPPOSITE
The deceptively simple, shedlike Lone Mountain Ranch House sits on a 27,000-acre cattle ranch in the high desert landscape of New Mexico.

PAGES 122 THROUGH 125
Two bedroom wings straddle this central space, which contains the kitchen and living and dining spaces.

Photographs Peter Ogilvie

OPPOSITE
A passageway to the left of the battened cement fireplace leads to a cozy media room, which then opens onto one of two offices that are part of an expansive master bedroom suite that comprises one of the two bedroom wings.

ABOVE RIGHT
The opposite wing of the house is composed of five bedrooms, all of which open off this central hall.

BELOW RIGHT
The smaller of the two offices in the master bedroom suite.

PAGES 128 THROUGH 131
The central living space is enclosed by floor-to-ceiling glass panels on two sides, with the south-facing glass wall (pages 128 and 129) shielded from the desert heat by the deep overhang of the roof.

Photographs Peter Ogilvie

STUDIO MK27
MM HOUSE
BRAGANÇA PAULISTA, BRAZIL

Marcio Kogan, principal of the architecture firm Studio MK27, has developed a reputation for creating villas that are luxurious, exotic, and very much of the twenty-first century without abandoning the hallmarks of twentieth-century Brazilian modernism that Kogan so admires. In line with these principles, and located in Bragança Paulista, an affluent community north of sprawling São Paulo, which Kogan designed with Maria Cristina Motta, and with interiors by Diana Radomysler, the MM House is organized by the intersection of two perpendicular axes: one axis dedicated to the house's structure, and the other to the house's copious outdoor spaces. The center of these two axes is the proverbial and literal heart of the house, the veranda, a spectacular room that is covered yet not enclosed, and directly off of which a large terrace and adjacent pool are accessed to the east, and an expansive living and dining space is accessed to the north.

This terrace is the transition between interior and exterior, dividing the house into two volumes. The southern volume contains the garage and a TV room, while the northern volume serves as the "main" house. Here the main volume of the house is dominated by the living and dining rooms, contained within a single open space distinguished by a dramatic pitched, wood-clad ceiling that extends the entire length of the massive space. Concealed behind a freestanding wall of shelves is access to the bright and airy kitchen, and from there to utility rooms, a maid's room, and accommodations for the caretaker's family. Also concealed behind the freestanding wall in the main living space is access to a lone corridor that traverses the entire length of the rest of the house, which includes four bedroom suites and a palatially scaled master suite.

Above the linear series of void and volumes that compose the house is a grass-covered pitched roof, which acts as an insulator, helping to keep the house cool throughout the year. In fact, the architects' approach to climate is essential to the habitability of the house. With permanent cross ventilation, the atmosphere is inviting, despite the high temperatures of the house's location in southeastern Brazil. Throughout the house, rooms are naturally ventilated through wooden folding doors and brise-soleils that can be fully opened, and which alternately give the front and rear facades a sense of warmth, protection, and transparency.

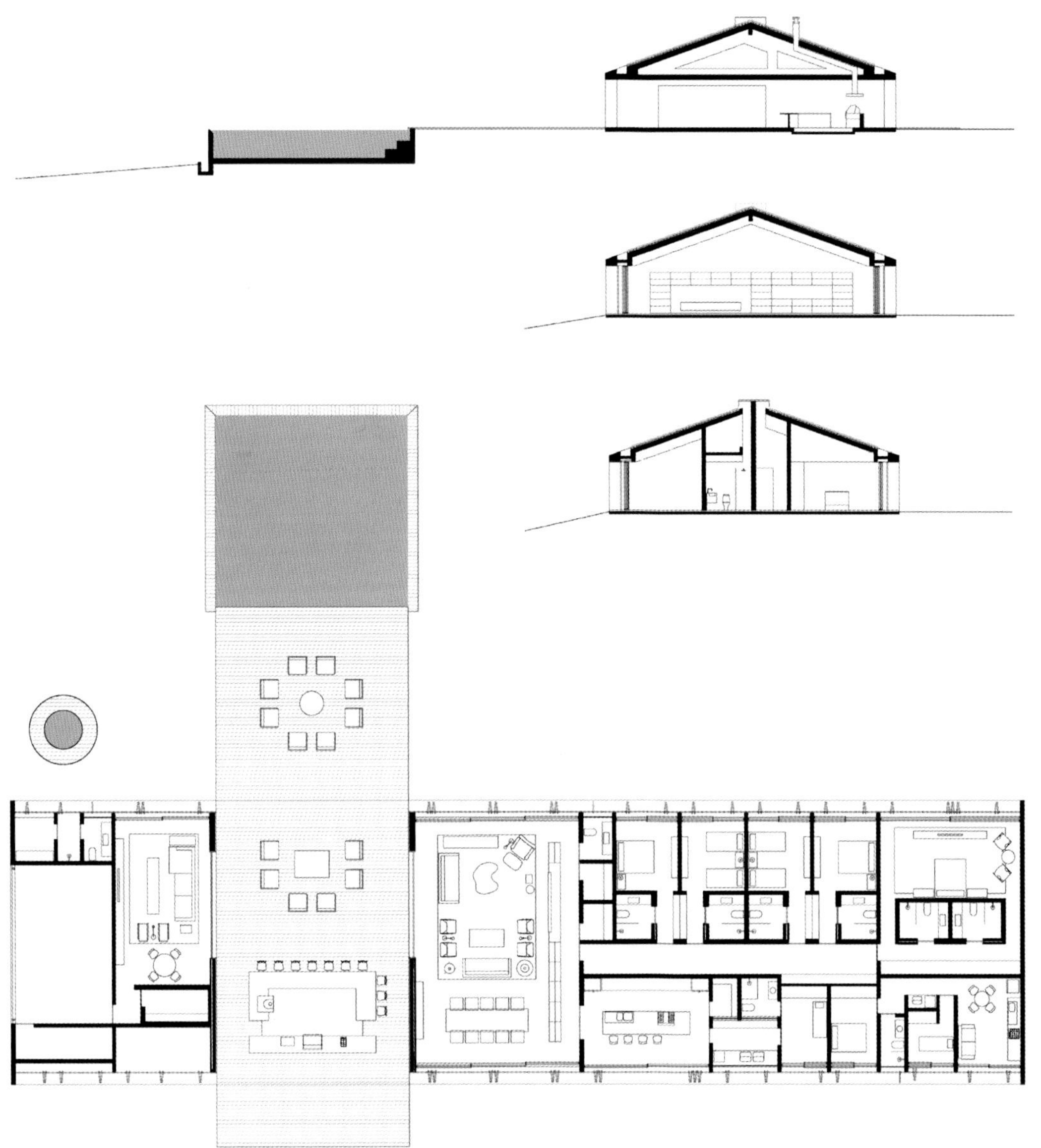

OPPOSITE AND FOLLOWING PAGES
The heart of MM House is the veranda, a spectacular room that is covered yet not enclosed.

ABOVE LEFT
The house was designed for entertaining, as the full bar in the veranda demonstrates.

BELOW LEFT
A view from the living room to the veranda.

OPPOSITE
A freestanding wall of shelves extends the length of the living and dining rooms, concealing the kitchen and the corridor to the house's bedrooms.

FOLLOWING PAGES
The living and dining rooms are contained within a single open space covered by a dramatic pitched, wood-clad ceiling.

ABOVE
Along the lengths of both sides of the house, wooden folding doors provide natural ventilation when open (left) and a sense of protection and warmth when closed (right).

OPPOSITE
In the dining room colorful glass pendant lights hang from the pitched wooden ceiling.

BELOW
Like the rest of the house, the kitchen is bright and airy, even with the shuttered doors outside closed.

PAGES 146 AND 147
From across the perfectly square pool, one can see the grass-covered pitched roof, which acts as an insulator, helping to keep the house cool throughout the year.

PAGES 148 AND 149
An expansive outdoor terrace lies between the pool and the veranda.

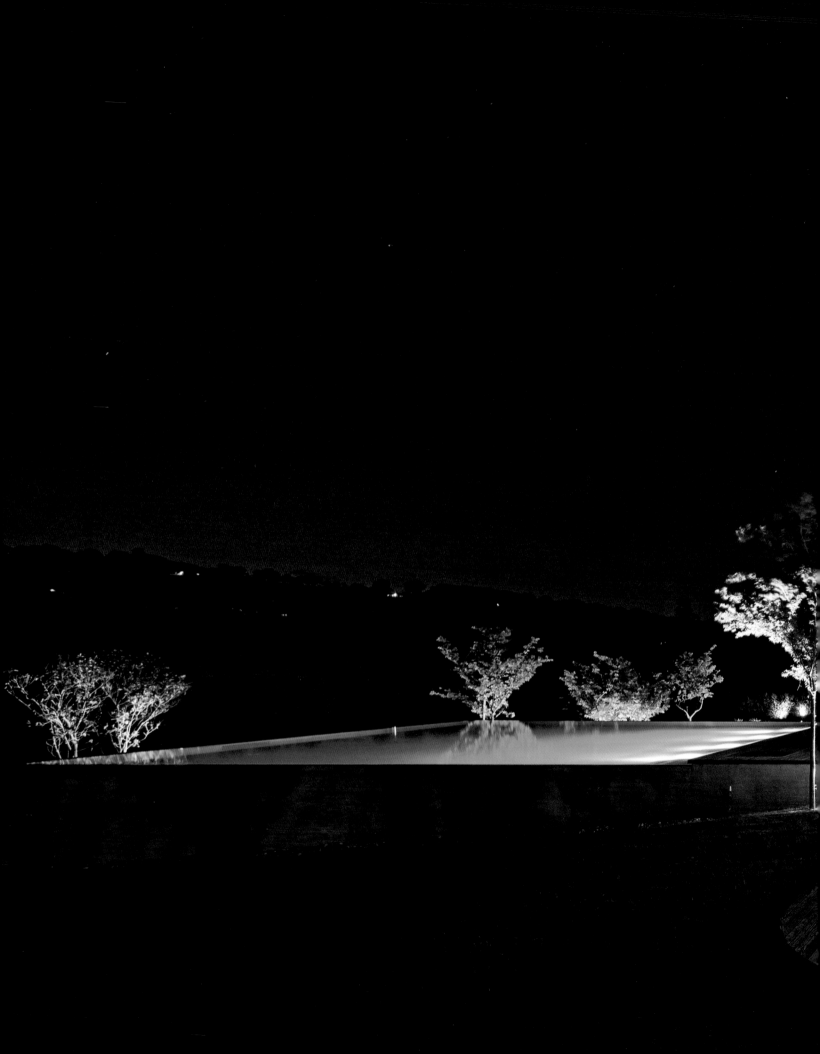

LAKE FLATO ARCHITECTS
DESERT HOUSE
SANTA FE, NEW MEXICO

San Antonio–based firm Lake Flato Architects has long been devoted to environmental sustainability in design, and this expansive, low-slung compound for two art collectors falls firmly in line with that ethos. The residence was conceived as a series of pavilions oriented around a courtyard and comprising the main house, two guesthouses—one a separate structure and one above the garage—and a long, narrow structure housing an indoor pool. Throughout the project, passive solar design strategies include the orientation of the house's floor-to-ceiling and clerestory windows to minimize heat gain during the summer and radiant-heated concrete floors to maximize warmth during the winter. Additionally the master bedroom suite and the separate guesthouse are both earth-sheltered, creating cocooned environments of maximum insulation against heat gain while contributing to the overall low profile of the structures in the landscape.

Rough materials of exposed concrete and rusted corrugated metal siding contrast with the refined and airy interior, especially in the so-called "great room," containing expansive living and dining space, and the adjacent long, narrow gallery, where the pristine white walls, polished concrete floors, and meticulously designed lighting give one the sense of occupying a small but exquisitely realized museum. According to the architects, the core condition underpinning the design of the house was the contradictory program of providing gallery-quality interior spaces while at the same time taking advantage of the expansive views in the high desert landscape of Santa Fe.

The architects characterize the art collection as the driving force of the "interior landscape" of the rooms. Along with the gallery, the main room provides for the display of art on the side walls of the long, high space while also allowing spectacular views to the east and west through glass walls protected from the desert southwest heat by the shade-producing roofs of the "sunrise" porch, off the main living area, and the "sunset" porch, off the kitchen, at either end of the structure.

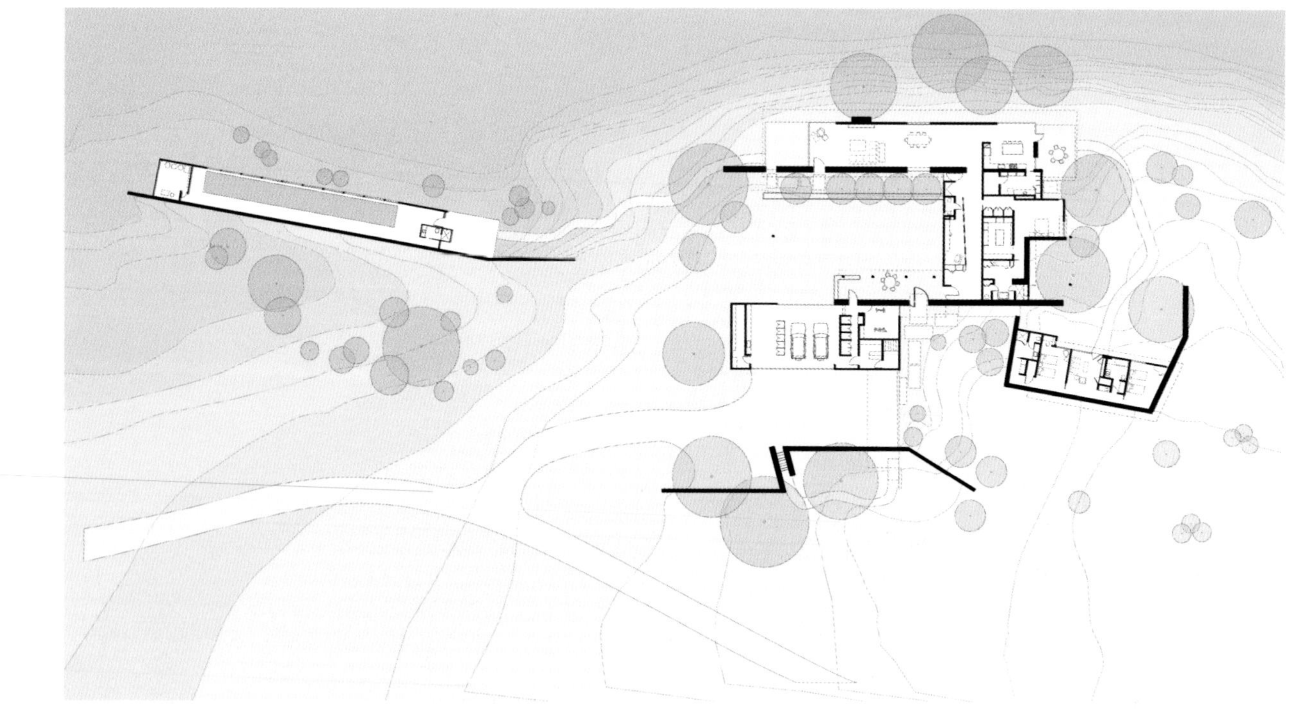

OPPOSITE
A view of the main house with one of two guesthouses in the foreground.

FOLLOWING PAGES
The "sunset" porch, which opens off the kitchen, is complemented by a "sunrise" porch off the living space at the opposite end of the house.

Manet
VAN GOGH IN ARLES
THE GARDENS OF JAPAN
KANDINSKY
MODERN WOMEN!
Gauguin
THE CITIES BOOK

OPPOSITE
Though it is bright and cheerful, the master bedroom suite is situated in the house so that it is extremely secluded from the other rooms.

ABOVE RIGHT
The long corridor to the master bedroom suite is lined with bookshelves on one side and built-in wardrobes on the other.

BELOW RIGHT
The detached guesthouse also serves as a gallery-like venue for the house's art-collector clients.

FOLLOWING PAGES
A large steel and steel-mesh gate opens onto a courtyard, with the front door to the house to the immediate right of the gate.

ABOVE
The entry foyer leads directly to the house's formal gallery.

FOLLOWING PAGES
Along with the gallery, the "great room," containing expansive living and dining space, also offers copious space for the display of art, giving one the sense of being in a small but exquisitely realized museum.

THAM & VIDEGÅRD
SUMMERHOUSE
NORRA LAGNÖ, SWEDEN

Since founding their Stockholm-based firm in 1999, Bolle Tham and Martin Videgård have developed a body of work that can be described as simultaneously pared down and aesthetically inventive. Paradoxical as that may sound, their projects, particularly residential, employ basic volumetric forms and simple, rational plans in tandem with unexpected materials and ironic intentions that subvert the expectations raised by the simplicity on their surfaces. The Summerhouse in Norra Lagnö, Sweden, is fully in line with this ethos.

Set on the south end of an island in the Stockholm archipelago, the house occupies a largely open site that slopes gently down to the Baltic seashore. The project was commissioned by a family seeking a vacation house that would distinguish itself from the light-constructed wooden cottage typical of the region. The architects' response was to propose poured-in-place concrete as visual reference to the site's granite bedrock rather than making any obvious allusion to the site's sylvan qualities.

The house is composed of two structures, together comprising 1,500 square feet: the main house, supporting three gables, and a single-gabled guest cottage. The two structures are aligned and connected by a fifth gable that is a transparent glass canopy spanning the open space between them. The result is a distinct yet simple formal profile determined by a series of five transverse gable roofs, which are an oblique reference to the boathouses for fishing vessels that once dominated the island's sparsely built landscape.

Each of the gables is of varying height and width, providing a sequence of correspondingly varying dimensions for the simple spaces beneath them in the main house: entry foyer, bathroom, kitchen, and three bedrooms. All of these rooms open by way of sliding wood panels directly onto the main living and dining space, which spans the entire length of the main structure and accesses an outdoor seashore-facing terrace via a continuous series of sliding glass partitions. The potential severity of such a repetition-based cast-concrete structure is modulated by the ash panels separating the bedrooms and service rooms from the main living space, by the teak frames surrounding the immense floor-to-ceiling sliding glass panels, and by the division of space in the main living area implied by the varied sequence of peaked ceilings above.

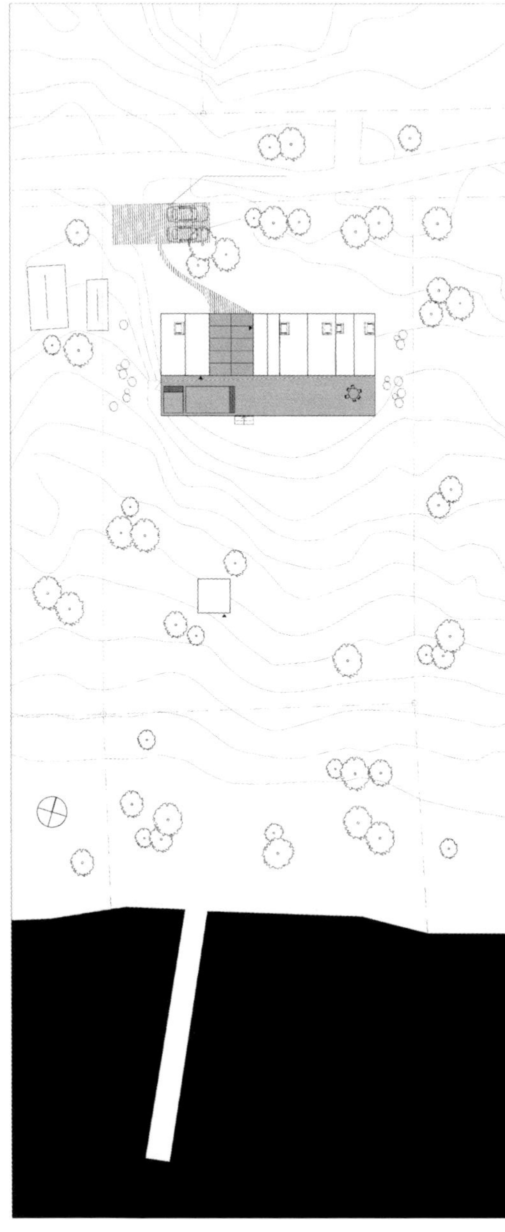

OPPOSITE
The house is set on the south end of an island in the Stockholm archipelago, occupying a largely open site that slopes gently down to the Baltic seashore.

FOLLOWING PAGES
The house is composed of the main structure, supporting three gables, and a single-gabled guesthouse, connected by a fifth gable that is a transparent glass canopy.

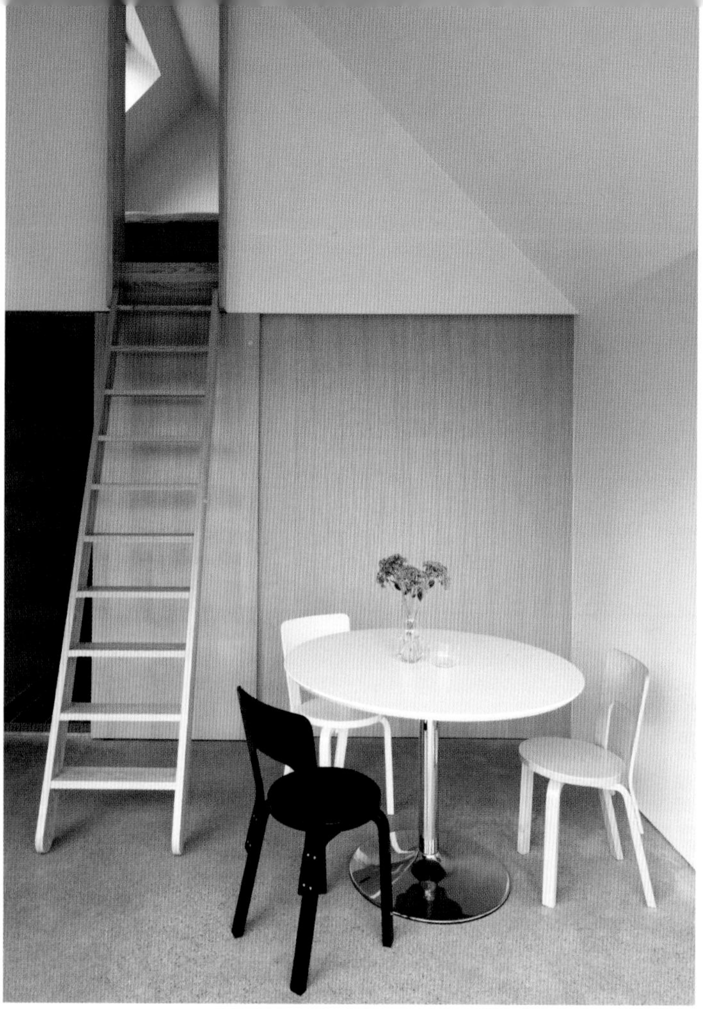

ABOVE LEFT
The compact guesthouse features a sleeping loft in its single gable.

BELOW LEFT
The kitchen in the main house is a simple galley plan, but the skylight and wood-framed picture window make it an inviting space.

OPPOSITE
An open living and dining space spans the entire length of the main house, while three bedrooms, the kitchen, and a bathroom are concealed behind sliding ash wood panels that appear as a single wall when closed.

PAGES 172 AND 173
In the main living and dining space, teak frames surround the immense floor-to-ceiling sliding glass panels, which access an outdoor terrace facing the sea.

PAGES 174 AND 175
While the lakeside facade of the house is dominated by glass, the house's opposite facade is virtually pure poured-in-place concrete, a response to the clients' request to avoid any obvious reference to the site's sylvan qualities.

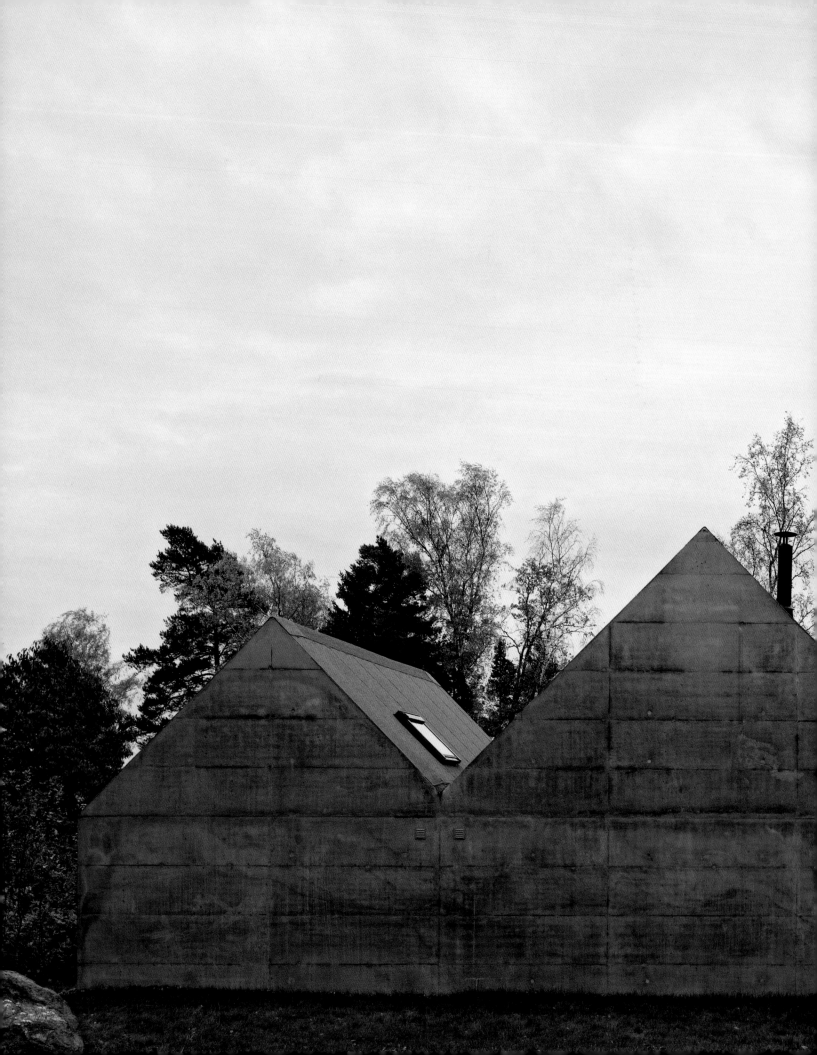

ATELIER OSLO
NORDERHOV CABIN
NORDERHOV, HØNEFOSS, NORWAY

This project, commissioned as a vacation house for a couple based in Oslo, is located in the Krokskogen forests, outside the town of Hønefoss. Sited on a steep slope, it offers a sweeping view of the lake Steinsfjorden. With a few simple but remarkably bold gestures, the young firm Atelier Oslo, established in 2006, has created a transfixing weekend house that, from the approach to its entrance, appears as an assemblage of angular wooden pavilions. Inside, the apparent agglomeration of volumes reveals itself to be a sinuous network of curved-wall, womblike spaces that effectively form one continuous room. Adding to the singular character of this residence is the near absolute openness on its lakeside facade, where floor-to-ceiling plate-glass walls offer a striking contrast to the blank solidity of the house's entry facade.

The site is often exposed to strong winds, so the cabin is organized to provide protection from the wind while also providing abundant natural light. Contributing further to the house's formal power is the restrained, almost minimalist approach to materials. The curved interior walls and ceilings form continuous surfaces clad with birch plywood. Even more impressive than the sculptural walls is the carefully modulated variation in floor levels, which follows the site's terrain and divides the plan into several levels that define the different functional zones of the cabin.

Introducing a podlike circular fireplace on the main access level near the center of the house, the architects arranged all the living spaces around a very up-to-date version of the timeless hearth. Living room, kitchen and dining area, bedroom, and bathroom unfold around the hearth in an organic plan that allows for the different rooms to assume a variety of orientations toward the lake so that a multiplicity of views is created. But just as the entry and lakefront facades of the house offer an object lesson in contrast, so does the supple execution of the interior wooden contours and frameless glazed walls oppose the primitivist impulse at the heart of this small but ambitious project.

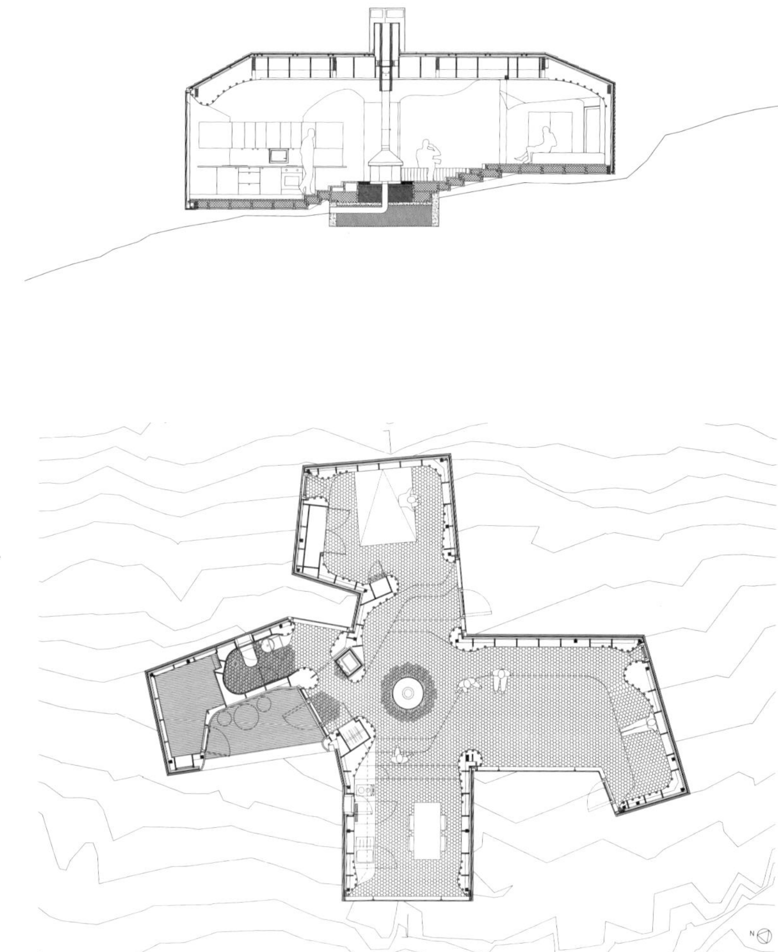

OPPOSITE
The cabin is sited on a steep slope, offering a fantastic view of the lake Steinsfjorden through floor-to-ceiling plate-glass walls.

FOLLOWING PAGES
The cabin's living spaces are arranged around a podlike circular fireplace, a very up-to-date version of the timeless hearth.

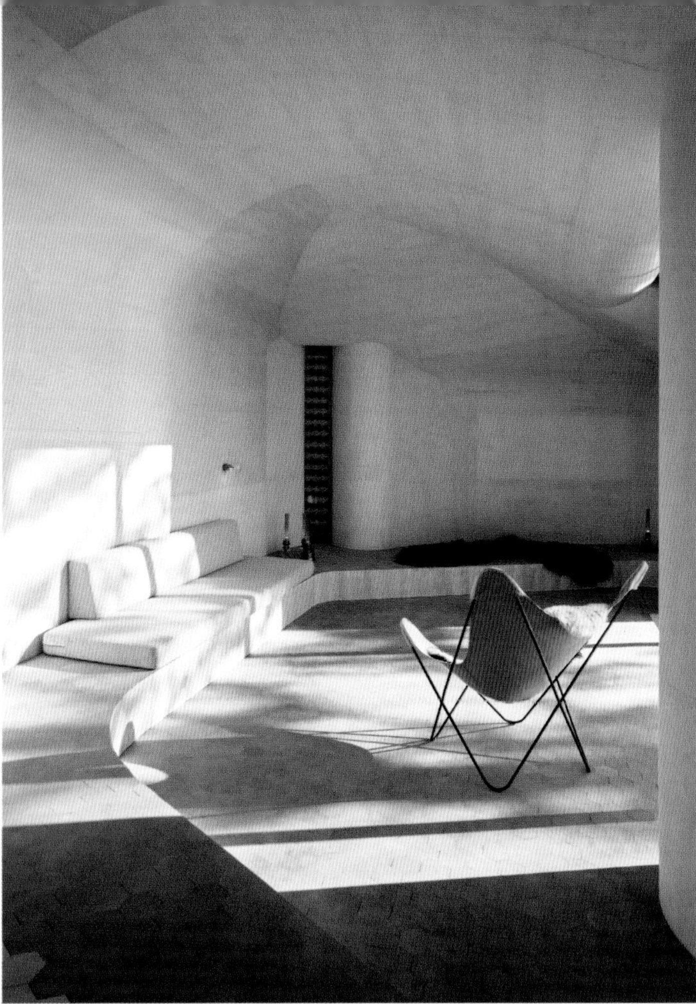

ABOVE LEFT
Inside, the curved walls and ceilings form continuous surfaces clad with birch plywood.

BELOW
A sinuous network of curved-wall, womblike spaces effectively form one continuous room, as seen in this view toward the kitchen to the left and the bedroom to the right of the central fireplace.

OPPOSITE
Carefully modulated variation in floor levels follows the site's terrain and divides the plan into several elevations that define the different functional zones of the cabin.

PAGES 184 AND 185
The site is often exposed to strong winds, so the cabin is organized to provide shelter from the wind, while strategically placed windows receive the sun at different times of the day, as with the dark-paned bathroom window within a deep exterior niche.

PAGES 186 AND 187
From the approach to its entrance, the cabin appears as an assemblage of angular wooden pavilions.

CHURTICHAGA + QUADRA-SALCEDO ARQUITECTOS
HOUSE IN SEGOVIA
SEGOVIA, SPAIN

Madrid-based architects Josemaria de Churtichaga and Cayetana de la Quadra-Salcedo owned a fairly isolated plot of land in rural Segovia for twelve years before they were ready to build their vacation house there. The architects let the natural hillside landscape dictate the form for this modestly scaled, timber weekend house. With idyllic views both up and down the hill, the site allowed them to create a two-story structure, with the main level above featuring two large decks on either side of an open living space. The massive span of the decks gives the appearance of a cantilevered plinth, below which the house's more compact lower level is nestled partially underground into the hillside.

The house is simply and clearly organized on two levels. The interior of the main floor is divided into three zones by a wide wall containing niches for a kitchen, storage space, and a fireplace facing the main living zone, where glass walls on two sides open onto the massive cantilevered decks. The entire area is devoted to comfortable living and dining space, with a compact kitchen tucked into a niche in one wall, and a fireplace and concealed storage space tucked into the opposite wall. To either side of the kitchen are two doors, one leading to an ingeniously compact master bedroom suite, and the other leading down a short corridor past a set of stairs to the lower level and onto the house's main entrance. In symmetrical fashion, doors to either side of the fireplace lead to a pair of narrow, cabinlike rooms for the couple's children.

The house's lower level comprises a long family room, with its own door leading outside, and a study, with both of these semi-subterranean rooms naturally illuminated by long, single-paned clerestory windows. Throughout the house, on both levels, pine boards or panels face every surface—wall, floor, and ceiling—giving a sense of warmth to the rational and compact series of spaces as well as fully integrating the house with its bucolic setting.

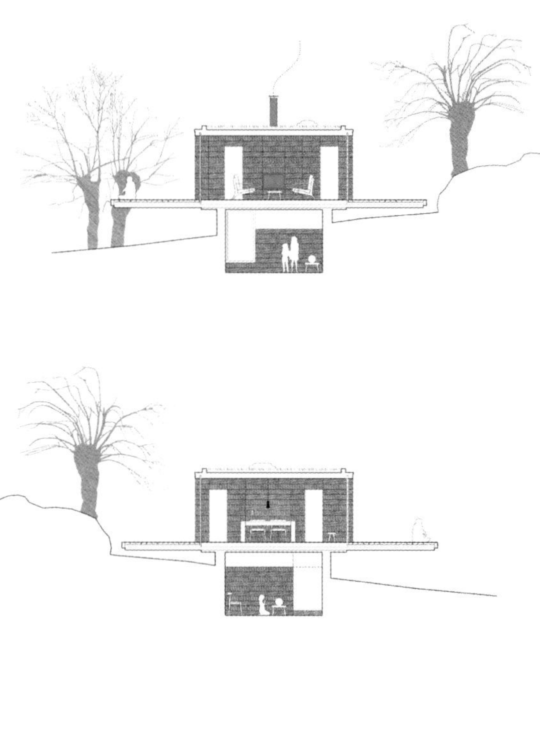

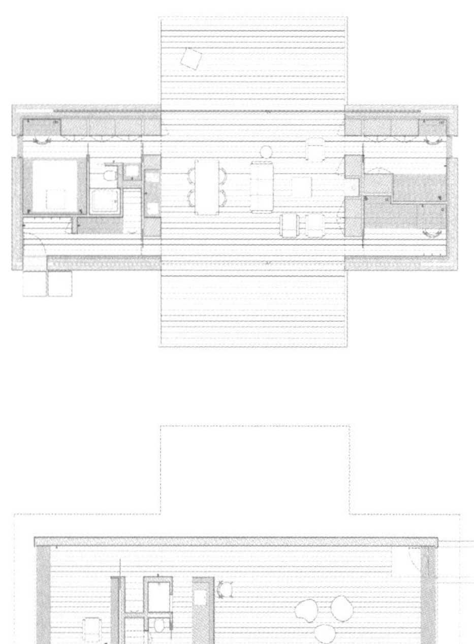

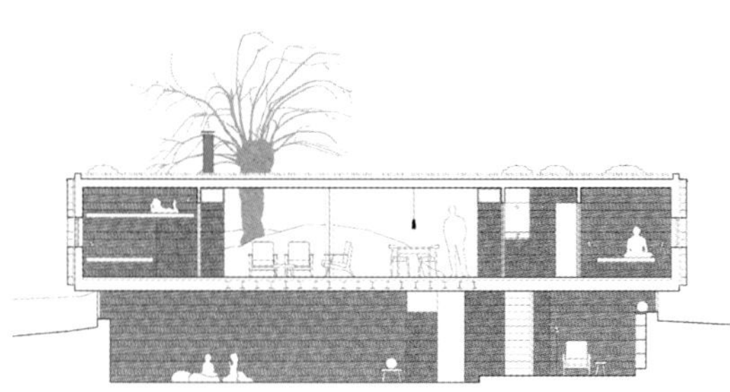

OPPOSITE
Throughout the house, pine boards or panels face every surface—wall, floor, and ceiling—as seen here in the house's main living space.

FOLLOWING PAGES
The site inspired the architects to create a two-story structure, with the main level above featuring two large decks on either side of the open living space.

BELOW
The architects let the natural hillside landscape dictate the form for the modestly scaled, timber weekend house, with its lower level nestled partially underground into the hillside.

OPPOSITE
The partially subterranean study receives natural light from a ground-level clerestory window.

FOLLOWING PAGES
The pine boards used unremittingly on virtually every surface of the house provide a powerful sense of warmth.

OPPOSITE
The massive span of the outdoor decks gives the appearance of a cantilevered plinth, reinforcing the formal austerity of the house's profile in the landscape.

ABOVE AND BELOW RIGHT
In addition to the study, the house's lower level accommodates a generously proportioned family room.

FOLLOWING PAGES
The children's bedrooms (left) and the master bedroom (right), receiving natural illumination only through skylights, are as ingeniously compact as a train compartment or ship's cabin.

FOUGERON ARCHITECTURE
FALL HOUSE
BIG SUR, CALIFORNIA

Though Anne Fougeron's firm, Fougeron Architecture, is known for a variety of project types, the clients for the Fall House, in Big Sur, were inspired to approach the architect thanks to another of Fougeron's residential projects, also in Big Sur. This house impressed the clients for the Fall House with Fougeron's solution to site the earlier house deep within a steep valley so that it was paradoxically conspicuous by virtue of its isolation. As Fougeron has written, "Placing form on wilderness is a radical act," an attitude that appealed to the clients of this three-bedroom vacation house on a breathtaking bluff along the Pacific Coast.

Fougeron found the most challenging aspect of the project was to maintain a balance between the inevitable transformation of the site to accommodate the house while still respecting, if not quite deferring to, the site. In order to achieve this, Fougeron made the house cling to the site in a linear structure that conformed to the bluff's crags and contours, creating a form that zigzags down the site to end at a master bedroom suite cantilevered over the ocean. The structure is clad in copper and glass, and maintains a low profile on the landscape.

Completely invisible from Highway 1, the house is composed of a tripartite plan, where two solid volumes are connected by a conservatory-like glass library. The highest of the two remaining volumes serves as the house's point of entry leading to an open space containing living and dining areas and the kitchen, all of which open onto a south-facing terrace shielded from the region's strong northwest winds. A staircase of ceremonial proportions leads down to the double-height library, enclosed by glass on the house's north and south facades and on the ceiling, while its east and west walls feature high-rising shelves and a fireplace. To either side of the staircase's landing are two guest bedrooms, while traversing through the library leads to the master bedroom suite, where the library's glass ceiling extends to cover the master bathroom. The master bedroom is the culmination of the promenade through the main rooms, rewarding those who enter with a sublimely vertiginous view of the Pacific Ocean.

In addition to a series of ambitious construction methods to achieve all of these effects, not to mention protect against earthquakes and erosion, the house features a host of sustainable design strategies: the open floor plan at multiple levels creates a condition known as stack ventilation, allowing the exhaustion of hot air and intake of cool fresh air; radiant hydronics warm the limestone floors more efficiently than conventional forced-air systems; and insulated low-E (or low-emissivity) glass reduces solar gain during the summer and improves comfort during the winter without sacrificing views.

OPPOSITE
Architect Anne Fougeron once wrote, "Placing form on wilderness is a radical act," an attitude that appealed to the clients of this three-bedroom vacation house on a breathtaking bluff along the Pacific Coast.

FOLLOWING PAGES
The house clings to the site in a linear structure that conforms to the bluff's crags and contours, and is clad in copper and glass.

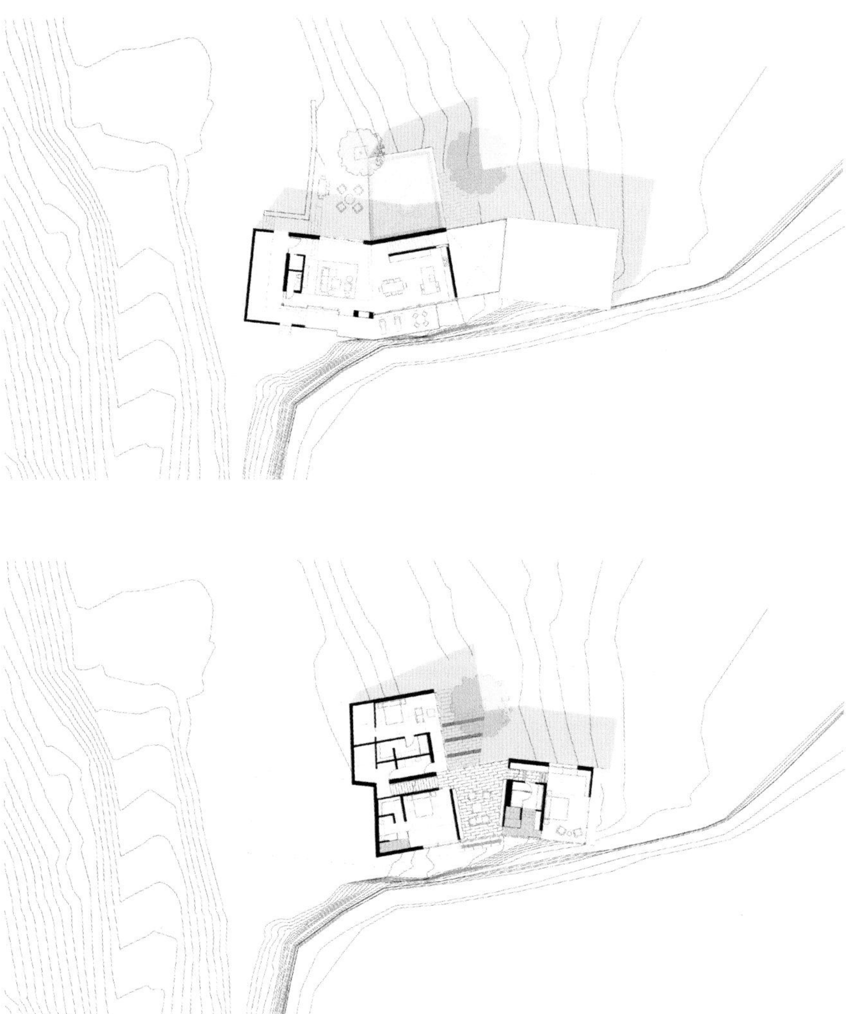

OPPOSITE
The house is composed of two levels, with an open living, dining, and kitchen space comprising the upper level.

PAGES 210 AND 211
A short flight of stairs down from the entry foyer leads to the living space, which opens onto a south-facing terrace shielded from the region's strong northwest winds.

PAGES 212 AND 213
The kitchen and dining space open onto a cantilevered terrace with a transparent parapet, offering breathtaking, if vertiginous, views north along the coast.

BELOW
The house's linear form zigzags down its steep site to culminate at the master bedroom suite, which is cantilevered over the oceanside bluff.

OPPOSITE
A tall partial wall exposes the adjacent library's glass ceiling to the master bathroom, which features a structurally elaborate yet formally minimalist tub composed of tile and glass.

OPPOSITE
A staircase of nearly monumental proportions leads to the double-height, glass-ceilinged library on the house's lower level.

BELOW
The view from the kitchen down to the voluminous library. Behind the freestanding wall with fireplace and bookshelves is a glimpse of the master bathroom and bedroom.

PAGES 218 AND 219
A series of ambitious construction methods was required to achieve protection against earthquakes and erosion on the precarious site.

PAGES 220 AND 221
A view into the library from another, more intimate south-facing terrace.

WILLIAM REUE
A HOUSE IN THE WOODS
UPSTATE NEW YORK

At the base of the Shawangunk Mountains, in a clearing among Norway spruces, sits a distinctly sculptural structure that, in the words of architect William Reue, is "the result of the studied relationship between two opposing geometries—a long sculptural wall clad in Cor-Ten weathering steel and a mass of stratified bluestone." Behind the sculptural wall of Richard Serra proportions, a modest entrance is a deceptively simple prelude to the breathtaking spaces to come, beginning with the living, dining, and kitchen space, an expansive open volume with a dramatic slanting ceiling and a wall composed entirely of floor-to-ceiling glass panels, a striking contrast to the monolithic blankness of the entrance facade.

Reue echoed the exterior profile of the house by introducing a sculptural dimension to the house's organization, materials, and details. The fireplace is a perfectly proportioned niche within a massive, brilliant white wall modulated by complementarily proportioned etched lines, while the kitchen is concealed behind a wall of similarly etched white panels, as well as by an adjacent wall of dark wood panels, and a minimalist white volume that functions as a kitchen island.

Reue distilled the house into three discrete zones: the open living, dining, and kitchen space; an adjacent yet private master bedroom suite; and a suite of three guest bedrooms secluded from the rest of the house to the degree that they effectively function as a guesthouse, complete with their own sitting room with wet bar, as well as a private entrance.

Though the master bedroom suite lies immediately adjacent to the main living space, its privacy is ensured by an entrance niche and short corridor leading to the amply proportioned room, all of which is located behind the massively thick wall that accommodates the fireplace in the main living space. Both the master bedroom and master bathroom enjoy views from the same wall of floor-to-ceiling glass found in the house's public zone, taking full advantage of the house's idyllic forest setting.

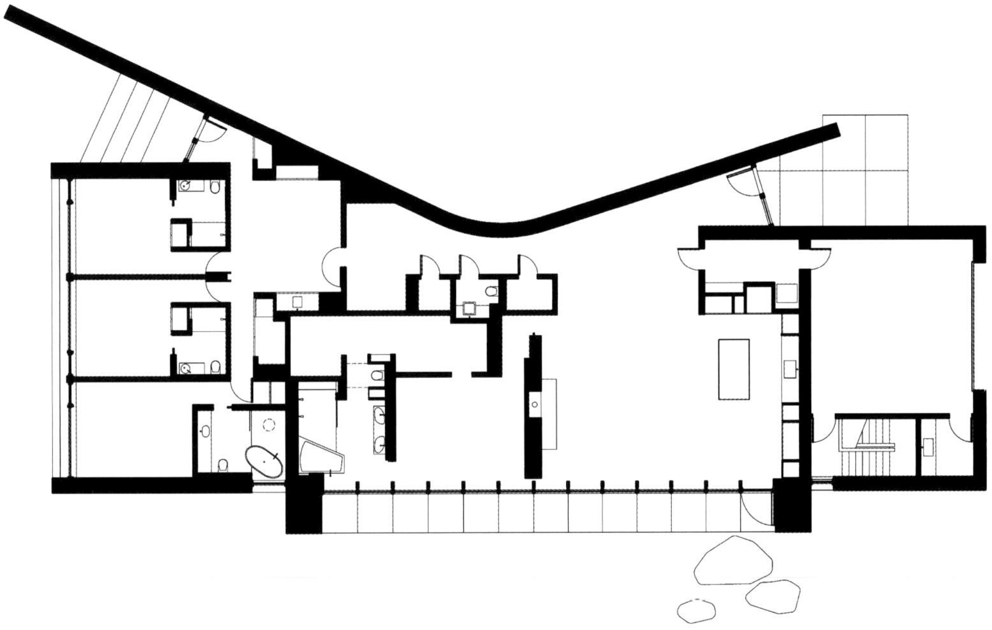

OPPOSITE
This house is a distinctly sculptural structure with a facade dominated by a long, curved wall of Richard Serra proportions, clad in Cor-Ten weathering steel.

PAGES 226 AND 227
Behind the steel wall, a modest entrance leads to the breathtaking living, dining, and kitchen space, an expansive open volume with a dramatic slanting ceiling and a wall composed entirely of floor-to-ceiling glass panels.

PAGES 228 AND 229
The kitchen is concealed behind a wall of white-paneled cabinets, in the background, as well as by an adjacent wall of dark wood panels, to the left. A sculpturally minimalist white volume functions as a kitchen island.

PAGES 230 AND 231
In the living space the fireplace is a perfectly proportioned niche within a massive, brilliant white wall modulated by complementarily proportioned etched lines. The short, narrow corridor to the immediate right of the wall leads to the secluded master bedroom suite.

OPPOSITE AND BELOW
Thanks to the house's isolated site, both the master bedroom and master bathroom enjoy views from the same wall of floor-to-ceiling glass found in the house's public areas.

FOLLOWING PAGES
On the approach to the house, sited at the base of the Shawangunk Mountains, in a clearing among Norway spruces, the facade maintains an exquisitely sculptural profile.

JOHN WARDLE ARCHITECTS
FAIRHAVEN BEACH HOUSE
FAIRHAVEN, AUSTRALIA

The Fairhaven Beach House is located at the top of the ridgeline above the Victorian coastline, a site that enjoys panoramic views over the Southern Ocean and beach below. Yet the orientations and dimensions of the house's windows have been tailored to particular views of the breathtaking seascape, and sometimes to reveal interior spaces to one another. Rather than emphasize the panoramic views natural to the site, the design process, according to the architect, was more akin to the art of scenography, integrating spatial experiences to create a series of frames from which to enjoy a multitude of views.

The house is carefully divided into zones to allow for privacy and communal gathering. Entry to the house is at an intermediate level, which contains a pair of bedrooms and a bathroom. The long entry sequence ends at a staircase leading down to the main public spaces—composed of living and dining spaces and kitchen—which are arranged to take advantage of particular views or to offer maximum protection from the elements by creating a central courtyard.

Once at the end of the dramatically compressed entry hall, a set of stairs leads down to reveal the expansive living space as well as the first glimpse of one of the house's many spectacular views. The main living space is separated from the combined dining and kitchen space by a fireplace mounted on a black granite plinth. The upper level houses a suite of private rooms, including a master bedroom and bathroom, a large private terrace, and, up one final set of stairs, a study that is partially open to the long entry hall and cantilevers over part of the central courtyard. A garage, laundry, and informal living space are hidden from view in a basement level.

A simple but bold material palette modulates the strong, angular profile throughout the house's interior as well as exterior. Zinc cladding is dramatically contrasted with large timber-framed panes of glass outside, while inside wood wall panels and ceilings comprise virtually the sole interior material, conveying a distinct sense of warmth rather than dominance.

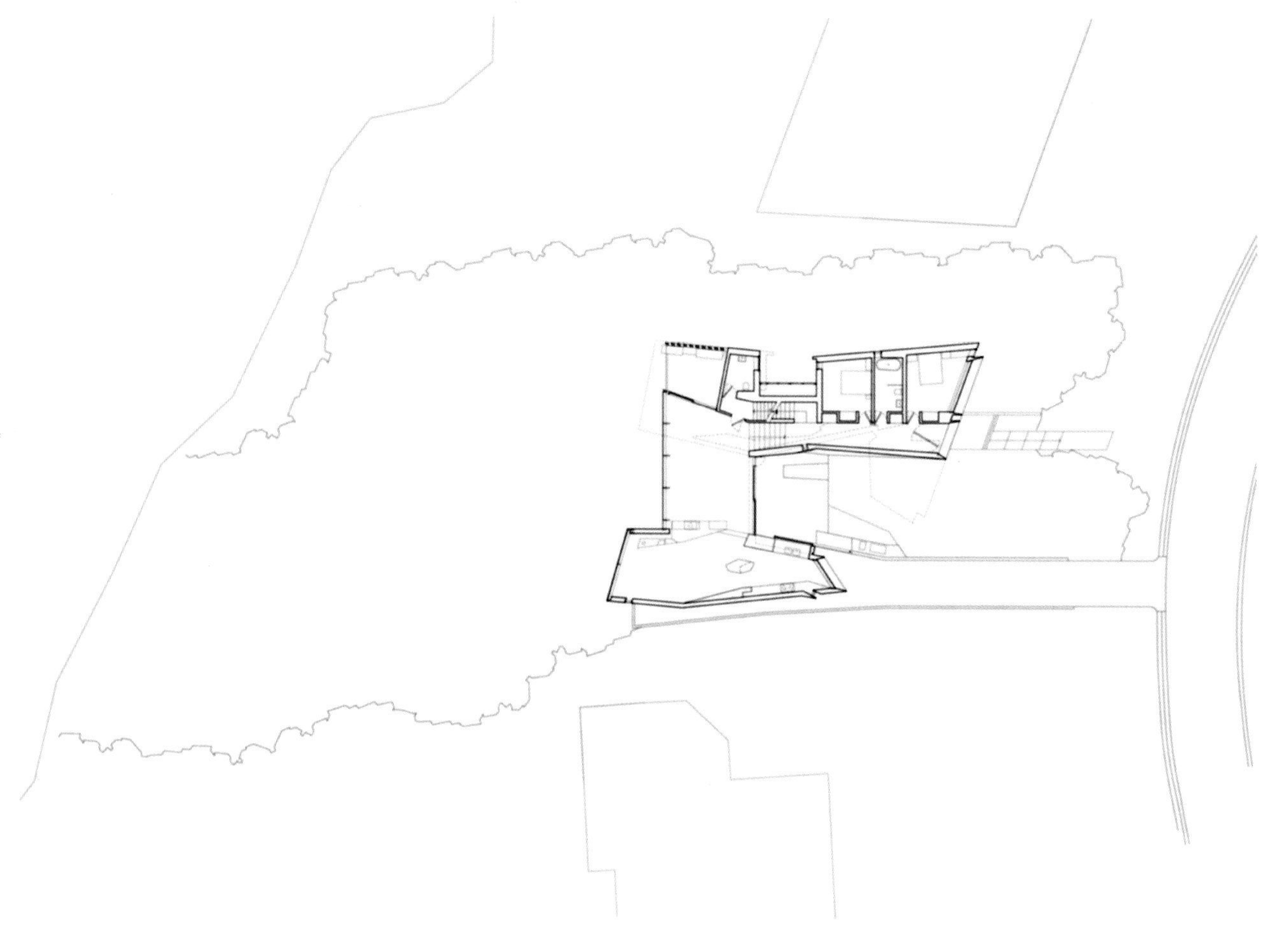

OPPOSITE
Entry to the house is at an intermediate level, where a long entrance sequence ends at a wide staircase leading down to the main living spaces and a winding staircase leading up to the master bedroom suite.

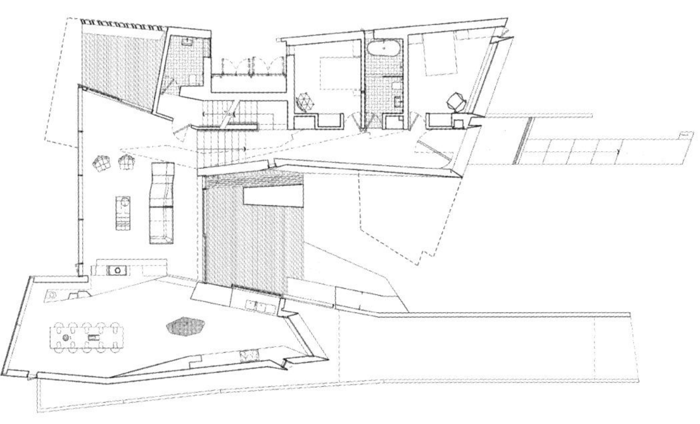

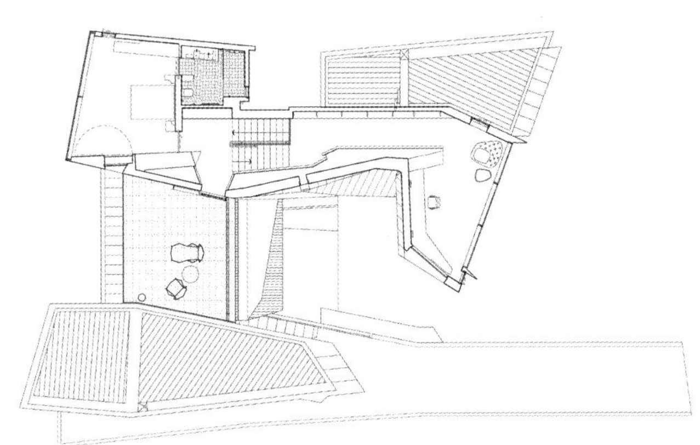

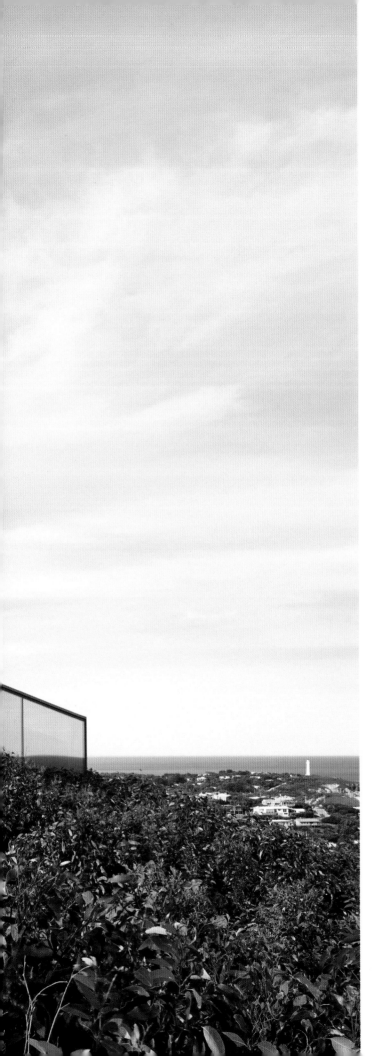

LEFT
The complex geometries of the house's entrance facade are contrasted by the relatively straightforward glass facades facing the ocean.

PAGES 242 AND 243
The house's windows have been tailored to particular views that not only capture the breathtaking seascape but also reveal interior spaces to one another. Wood-framed sliding panels open the living room (right) and the kitchen (left) to the house's central courtyard.

PAGES 244 AND 245
The main living space, which enjoys views of the ocean as well as access to the courtyard, is separated from the combined dining and kitchen space by a fireplace mounted on a black granite plinth.

OPPOSITE
The polygonal front door pivots rather than swings open onto the long entry corridor, off of which are two bedrooms.

BELOW
The tilted wall on the west side of the entry corridor gives the space a sculptural quality, which is reinforced by the very narrow overlook from the long mezzanine above.

PAGES 248 AND 249
The kitchen and dining room compose one large, sinuous space ideal for casual entertaining.

PAGES 250 AND 251
The master bedroom is an object lesson in minimalism, not only because of the uniform wood cladding, which appears throughout the house, but thanks to such touches as concealed built-in drawers and wardrobes and the neon blue built-in nightstands.

KIERANTIMBERLAKE
POUND RIDGE HOUSE
POUND RIDGE, NEW YORK

Philadelphia-based KieranTimberlake, headed by Stephen Kieran and James Timberlake, is emerging as one of the most lauded American architecture firms of the early-twenty-first century. Recent commissions include a new embassy building for the United States in London, a new mixed-use building for New York University, and the redesign of Philadelphia's JFK Plaza, home of Robert Indiana's famous LOVE statue. KieranTimberlake was also one of five architects invited to build houses as part of the Museum of Modern Art's landmark exhibition on prefabricated residential design.

However, unlike the firm's experiments in prefabrication, this house in Pound Ridge, New York, is a new construction very much inspired by and rooted in its particular site. According to the architects, the clients for this house expressed a desire for a "house in the woods, of the woods," and they set the house at the top of a boulder-strewn ridge on the site, which also contained the remnants of fieldstone farm walls dating from the nineteenth century. These walls were the inspiration for the stone used in the exterior material palette, which also includes tin-zinc-coated copper, brushed stainless steel, polished stainless steel, and glass, with the latter two giving the house a shimmering, otherworldly quality.

The house is organized as two volumes connected by a glass bridge. The front volume comprises two levels, the lower of which accommodates the house's main entrance, a garage, a workshop, a wine cellar, and mechanical spaces. The upper level, accessible by elevator as well as by a sculptural stone and wood staircase, comprises the house's private zone, including a den, two bedrooms, and a particularly spacious master bedroom, all organized along a single corridor. From this level one crosses a glass-enclosed bridge to a single-level volume containing an open living and dining space and kitchen, as well as a self-contained media room and a somewhat more open office.

In keeping with their ethos of environmentally sustainable design, KieranTimberlake employed tightly constructed Structural Insulated Panel (SIP) enclosures, which, along with wood-framed triple glazing, allow for a highly insulated building envelope. As a result, according to the architects, the house gains solar heat and retains it very efficiently during the winter, while during the warmer months apertures oriented for cross-ventilation greatly reduce the need for mechanical cooling. The overall effect is of a rustic yet luxurious villa that maintains an intensely poetic relationship to its surrounding landscape.

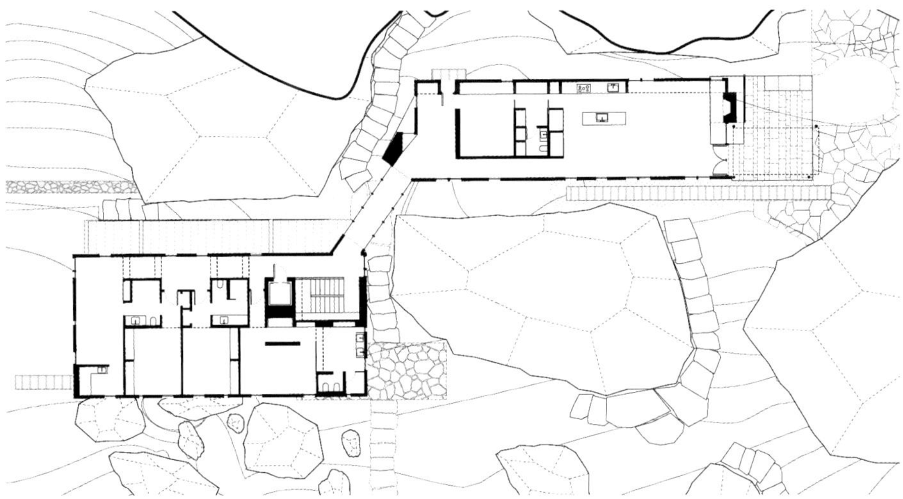

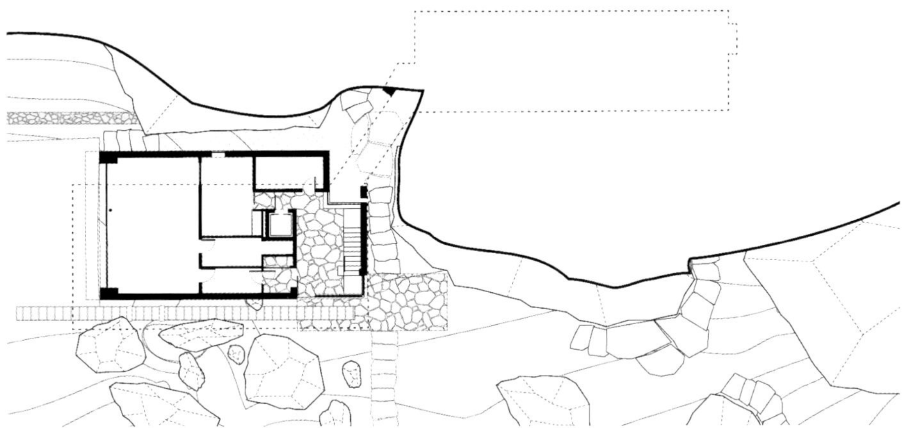

OPPOSITE
Remnants of fieldstone farm walls on the house's site dating from the nineteenth century were the inspiration for the stone used on the house's exterior.

OPPOSITE AND FOLLOWING PAGES
These views from inside (opposite) and from outside the open living, dining, and kitchen space demonstrate how the house satisfied the clients' desire for a "house in the woods, of the woods."

OPPOSITE
The house's two levels are connected by a sculptural stone and wood staircase, as well as by an elevator.

ABOVE AND BELOW RIGHT
Detail views of the alternating embedded stone and freestanding wood treads and the delicate curve of the balustrade as it meets the floor.

PAGES 262 AND 263
The house's rhythmic alternation of glass and solid walls both allows copious natural light to enter the rooms and provides surfaces on which the clients can display their collection of contemporary art.

PAGES 264 AND 265
Aside from stone, the material palette used on the exterior of the house includes tin-zinc-coated copper, brushed stainless steel, polished stainless steel, and glass, with the latter two giving the house a shimmering, otherworldly quality.

BATES MASI + ARCHITECTS
MOTHERSILL
WATER MILL, NEW YORK

Undoubtedly the most remarkable feature of this vacation home in the Hamptons is the presence of two small structures built by revolutionary architect Andrew Geller in 1962. The structures, a studio and a guesthouse, share an elevated wooden boardwalk, a feature that is not unique to the work of Geller and in fact is a regional touchstone in the local landscape, providing access from house to beach and, as with the Geller structures, sometimes from building to building.

Harry Bates, who resides in East Hampton, was in private practice in New York City for seventeen years before moving his firm to Southampton in 1980. Paul Masi, who joined the firm in 1998, spent childhood summers in Montauk and currently resides in Amagansett. So it was with considerable experience negotiating the built context and cultural landscape of the Hamptons that the architects approached this project, whose clients expressed their desire to integrate the new house with the Geller structures. To realize their clients' goals, Bates and Masi conceived of the construction of a circulation system that would link the various elements of the site in the form of a raised wooden path reminiscent of the boardwalks that connected the original Geller structures.

Siting the new house on a slope leading down to a creek, the architects arranged the house on two levels, with the first level largely devoted to a series of rooms that are discrete yet linked by a simple open circulation axis. With the exception of a hermetic bedroom zone at the end corner of the house, the ground level is a continuous promenade through a glazed entrance gallery to the living room on one side and the kitchen and dining area on the other. From there, two short open corridors on either side of the kitchen lead to the family room, then finally the promenade culminates in a long hall leading to the master bedroom and on to the two children's bedrooms.

Downstairs, two bedrooms, maid's quarters, a gym, and a recreation room are organized along a single corridor. Where the upper level was conceived in a spirit of openness, the lower level functions as a series of closed spaces that open directly onto the rear of the property, which slopes down to the creek. But the tour de force of the project is the boardwalk at the front of the house that leads from the Geller guesthouse, which was relocated, to a new swimming pool. And as before, the new boardwalk physically connects the Geller studio and guesthouse. As the path continues, passing the original studio structure—which now functions as a pool house—the route to the main house defines a central lawn, around which a series of open and covered outdoor spaces culminates in its connection to the main house, creating a compound of structures arranged with unerring elegance.

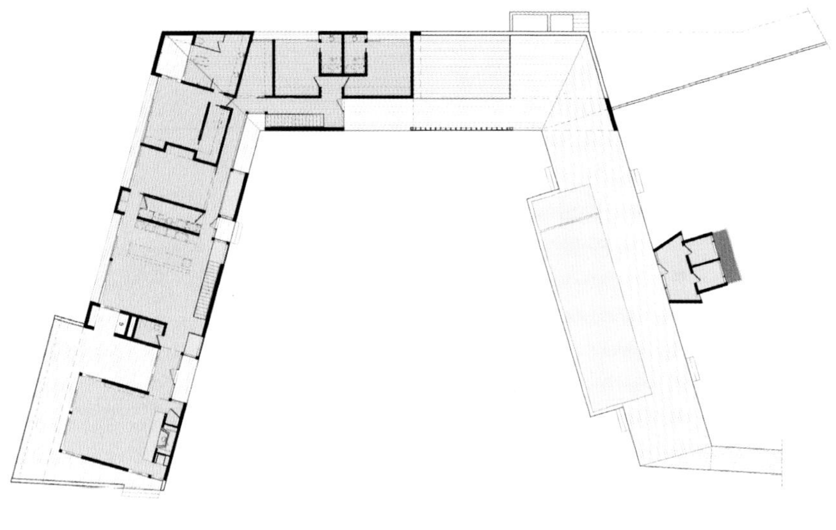

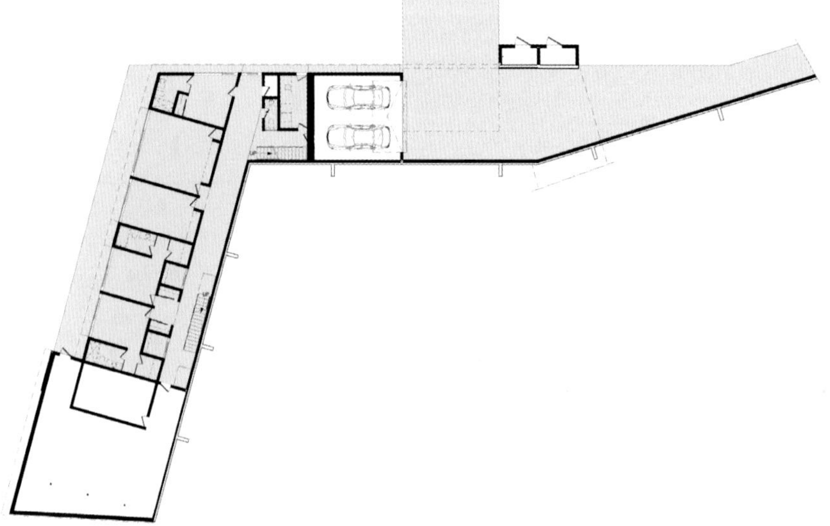

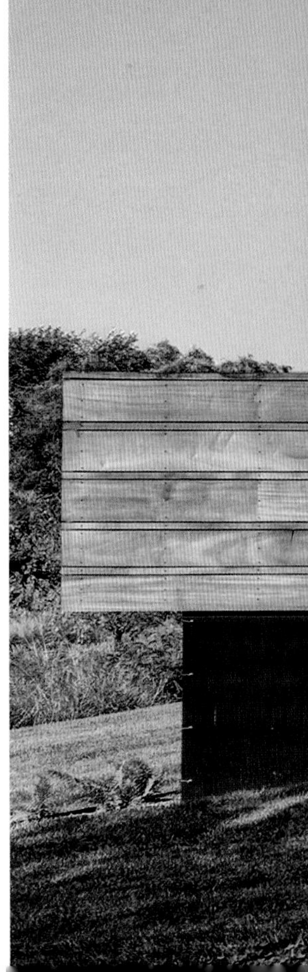

PAGE 266
The guesthouse is one of two small structures built by noted architect Andrew Geller on the property in 1962; the other is a studio that has been converted into a pool house.

OPPOSITE
At one end of the long, linear newly built structure is the living room, which, in addition to accessing a large terrace elevated over the hillside site, features a dramatic glass-enclosed niche that rises beyond the roof to the full height of the room's chimney.

FOLLOWING PAGES
The house's sole dining space is informal, sharing a room with the open kitchen, but large enough for entertaining.

BELOW
The house's extremely linear plan provides for a single corridor, to the right of the kitchen, which accesses the rest of the rooms on the upper floor: a family room, the master bedroom suite, and two children's bedrooms.

OPPOSITE
One of the children's bedrooms, which features cantilevered bunkbeds, built-in desk space, and massive single-paned picture windows.

ABOVE AND BELOW LEFT
The master bathroom is a paradoxical composition of warm wood, basalt stone, and abundant glass, with an outdoor shower just beyond the window adjacent to the freestanding tub.

OPPOSITE
Despite the monolithic, blackened steel fireplace that is the focal point of the space, the living room remains simultaneously airy and cozy.

PAGES 276 AND 277
The tour de force of the project is the boardwalk at the front of the house that leads from the Geller guesthouse, which was relocated, to a new swimming pool and to the main house beyond.

PAGES 278 AND 279
Siting the new house on a slope leading down to a creek, the architects arranged the structure on two levels. Where the upper level was conceived in a spirit of openness, the lower level functions as a series of closed spaces that all open directly onto the rear of the property.

TOM
FORD

PETER ROSE + PARTNERS
ISLAND RESIDENCE
EDGARTOWN, MASSACHUSETTS

This single-family residence by Boston-based Peter Rose + Partners defers to the surrounding wooded coast and wetlands, nestled into a narrow strip of land on the island of Chappaquiddick. The goal of the project was to create a residence emerging from and engaging with its surroundings, and providing ample entertaining and living space—both outdoor and indoor—for an active young family of five and their guests. By subtly raising the natural topography while at the same time lowering the house into the bluff, views are maximized while the building's presence is minimized. Meanwhile, the entry drive terminates at a garage and shed, which occupy an elevation completely below the site lines of the main house and are clad in naturally weathering cedar louvers and covered by green roofs planted with the same sea grasses as in the adjacent meadow.

At the main entry on the highest point of the landscape, a glass door reveals a view directly through the house to the Atlantic Ocean. Turning 180 degrees, one sees across the planted roofs of the sunken garage and shed to the waters of Cape Pogue Bay. Organized around an axis created by a long entry hall, the house is split into two zones. On one side a low, single-story living area includes kitchen, breakfast room, main dining room, and living room. On the other a compact, two-story volume includes seven bedrooms and four bathrooms arranged on two levels accessed by shallow, ramplike stairs.

Heavy, exposed Douglas fir beams carry flat roofs across the living spaces, supporting soil and plants above that improve thermal performance, reduce rainwater runoff, and allow the roofs to blend with the landscape. The wood supports are carried by wide flange steel beams, around which Douglas fir board-and-batten ceilings create a sense of warmth, richness, and comfort, as do the slate floor stone and Douglas fir tongue-and-groove wall planks. The large, mahogany-framed windows were made by an island craftsman and slide completely open so that the landscape and sea are a constant presence.

To minimize the house's environmental impact, multiple sustainability strategies are deployed in addition to the green roofs. All rooftop runoff is collected in a single mahogany gutter, visible from the breakfast room as it falls into a catchment basin surrounded by boulders. From there it is carried to an underground cistern for use in landscape irrigation and fire protection. All indoor spaces are warmed by efficient water-carried radiant heat, and ventilation is provided by the large sliding windows. And perhaps most ingeniously, the strategic location of native deciduous trees provides shade in the summer and allows solar gains in the winter.

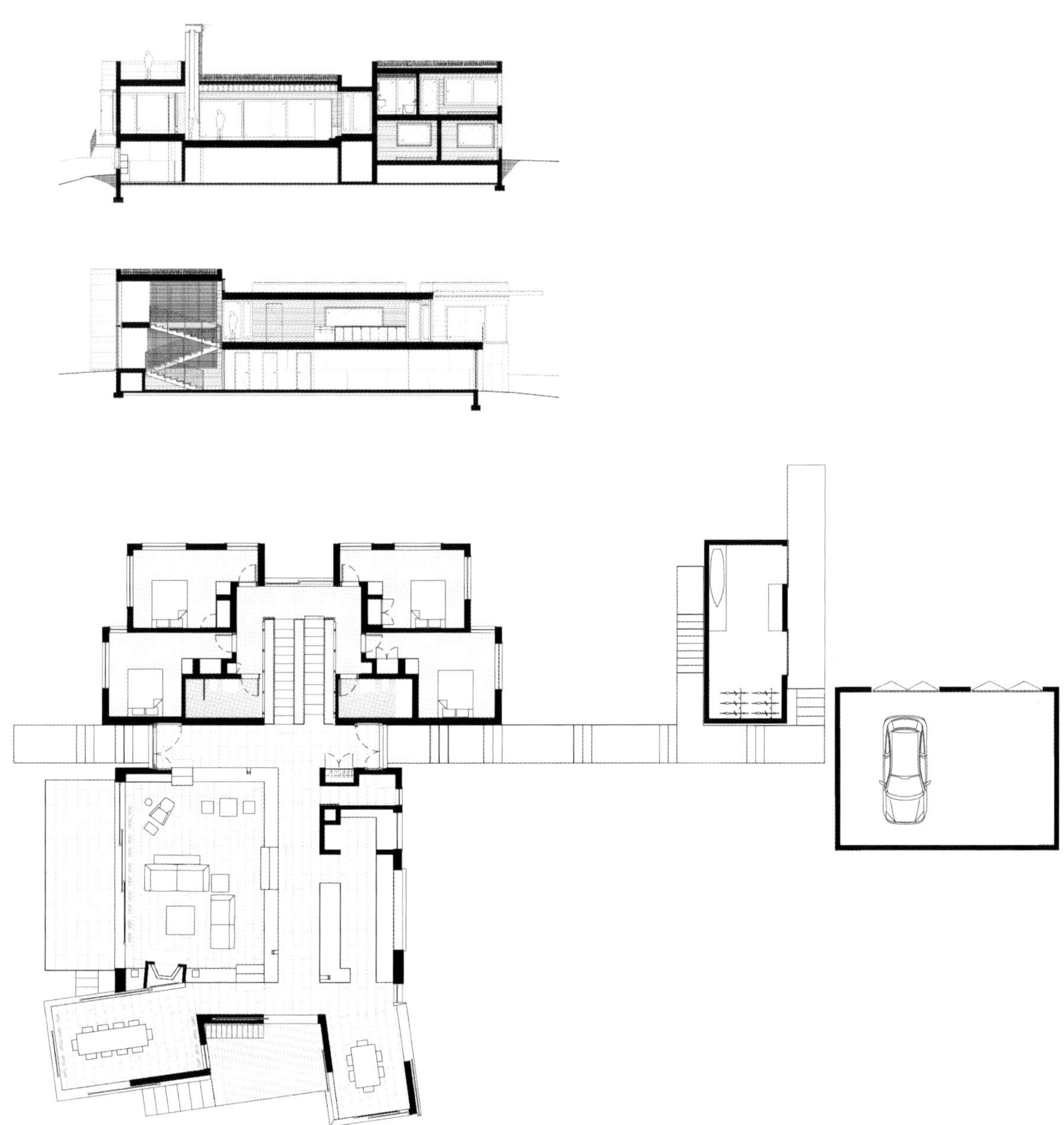

OPPOSITE
An axis created by a long entry hall divides the house into two zones: a low single-story living area, and a compact two-story volume containing the bedrooms.

PAGES 284 AND 285
The house's garage and shed occupy an elevation completely below the site lines of the main house and are clad in naturally weathering cedar louvers and covered by green roofs planted with the same sea grasses as in the adjacent meadow.

PAGES 286 AND 287
The zone containing the main living area includes a kitchen, breakfast room, living room, and more secluded dining room.

BELOW
The main living level is set midway between the two bedroom floors, raising the living spaces just enough to offer dramatic ocean views while at the same time making the building less obtrusive and more of a piece with the landscape.

OPPOSITE
Turning right from the main entry axis, a light, airy beech stair leads a half flight up or down to the two bedroom levels, and faces a two-story glass window that opens toward shrubbery and pine trees, and the adjacent open space preserve.

PAGES 290 AND 291
Throughout the house, windows are large, mahogany-framed lift and slides made by an island craftsman. In the dining room, the wood-framed glass slides out of the way on three sides, making the sight, sound, and smell of the sea a constant presence.

PAGES 292 AND 293
Heavy, exposed Douglas fir beams carry the flat roof across the open living space. The slate floor stone and Douglas fir tongue-and-groove wall planks provide a sense of permanence and warmth.

ABOVE
To minimize the environmental impact of the new construction, the residence deploys a suite of sustainability strategies that are integrated into the design of the building, including green roofs, a rainwater collection system, naturally ventilated facades, and hydronic radiant floors.

FOLLOWING PAGES
The living room and dining room, with their mahogany-framed doors slid completely open, create an idyllic vision of modern yet warm and nature-oriented domesticity.

ACKNOWLEDGMENTS

First, thank you to the architects and photographers whose brilliant work fills these pages. At Rizzoli International Publications I am grateful to publisher Charles Miers and associate publisher David Morton for their enthusiastic support, to Susan Lynch for her production expertise (particularly her wizardly skill with color proofs), to managing editor Lynn Scrabis for her willingness to always help find a solution, to Kayleigh Jankowski for her unwavering technical support, and to Victoria Brown for her eagle eye. Special thanks go to my editor, Alexandra Tart, for her skill and patience, and to graphic designer Claudia Brandenburg for creating an inspired layout that, for a second time, has made my efforts look good. I would also like to thank Matt Anderson at Olson Kundig Architects; Joel Sanders and Melissa LeBoeuf at OTTO; Rufus Knight at Fearon Hay Architects; Gabriel Fung at Herbst Architects; Ed Friel at Carl Turner Architects; Kelly Britton, Brent Linden, and Sarah Royalty Delph at Allied Works Architecture; Huan Zheng at Bercy Chen Studio; Meara Daly at Nelson Daly Communications; Michael Hatcher at Bohlin Cywinski Jackson; Nancy Wilson at Rick Joy Architects; Laura Guedes at Studio MK27; Sierra Haight and Cecilia Smith at Lake Flato Architects; Juan Ruiz at Atelier Oslo; Niraj Kapadia at Fougeron Architecture; Justine Makin and Amanda Ritson at John Wardle Architects; Carin Whitney at KieranTimberlake; Alana Leland at Bates Masi + Architects; and Christian Garland at Peter Rose + Partners.

PHOTOGRAPHY CREDITS

Page 2: Peter Aaron/OTTO
Pages 4–5: Matthew Snyder
Page 6: Joe Fletcher Photography
Page 8: Steve Freihon

THE PIERRE
Benjamin Benschneider/OTTO

ISLAND RETREAT
Patrick Reynolds

UNDER POHUTUKAWA
Patrick Reynolds

OCHRE BARN AND
STEALTH BARN
Carl Turner

DUTCHESS COUNTY
MAIN RESIDENCE
Pages 62, 65, 66–67, 68, 69, 70–71,
72, 73, 74: Jeremy Bitterman
Pages 75, 76–77: Jason Schmidt

EDGELAND HOUSE
Paul Bardagjy

TORO CANYON HOUSE
Laure Joliet

SKYLINE HOUSE
© Nic Lehoux

LONE MOUNTAIN RANCH HOUSE
Peter Ogilvie

MM HOUSE
Fernando Guerra

DESERT HOUSE
Frank Ooms

SUMMERHOUSE
Åke E:son Lindman/OTTO

NORDERHOV CABIN
Pages 176, 179, 180–81, 182, 183, 186–87:
Lars Petter Pettersen
Pages 184–85: Atelier Oslo

HOUSE IN SEGOVIA
Fernando Guerra

FALL HOUSE
Joe Fletcher Photography

A HOUSE IN THE WOODS
Steve Freihon

FAIRHAVEN BEACH HOUSE
Pages 236, 239, 242–43, 244–45, 246, 247,
248–49, 250–51: Trevor Mein
Page 240: Sean Fennessy

POUND RIDGE HOUSE
Peter Aaron/OTTO

MOTHERSILL
Bates Masi + Architects

ISLAND RESIDENCE
Courtesy Peter Rose + Partners

First published in the United States of America in 2015
by Rizzoli International Publications, Inc.
300 Park Avenue South
New York, NY 10010
www.rizzoliusa.com

2015 2016 2017 2018 / 10 9 8 7 6 5 4 3 2 1

Distributed in the U.S. trade by Random House, New York

Design by Claudia Brandenburg, Language Arts

Printed in China

ISBN-13: 978-0-8478-4599-6

Library of Congress Control Number: 2015934545